How To Build An Old Skool Bobber

Kevin Baas

Published by:
Wolfgang Publications Inc.
217 Second Street North
Stillwater, MN 55082
www.wolfpub.com

Legals

First published in 2006 by Wolfgang Publications Inc.,
217 Second Street North, Stillwater MN 55082

ISBN number: 1-929133-24-3

Printed and bound in Canada

How To Build An Old Skool Bobber

Acknowledgements

My first book, wow, what an experience. This journey has opened my eyes and allowed me to take a good look at how this bike industry has changed. The idea of building old skool styled bikes in class with my students has forever changed my life and has definitely put it's mark on the bike industry. To be given this opportunity to work on the book was a huge honor!

I would like to express my greatest thanks to Tim Remus and his crew at Wolfgang Publications. Without their help, support and guidance; I never would have gotten this project completed. What started as something I thought would be a piece of cake turned into many late nights and long weekends and lots of scrambling trying to get everything together. Tim, Jacki and the rest of the staff are top notch and have helped me in many ways through this project and I am deeply thankful for this.

To all the other builders, friends and mentors I thank you as well. Jeff and Donny at Sucker Punch Sally's have been supporters of my high school builds from the start and have the style of bikes this book is all about. Bret Smith, Bryan Conyers, Howard Kelly and James Simonelli at S&S have supported us from the beginning. Lee at Broadway Choppers, Weyland at Solutions Machining, Terry at Terry's Customs and George at Spartan Frameworks have all helped in a variety of ways. Thanks to all, not only for your support of the class builds, but also for putting up with my constant craving for information. To the Black Label Frameworks crew for filling their short notice request for frame and girder build photos, I appreciate your effort and willingness to help out. I'm grateful to Flyrite, for their cool retro styled bike pics and Ed Martin at Jammer for all his help. I would also like to give a big thanks to everyone who supported this project and to all the people who sent photos of your bikes. You know who you are and be assured I appreciate the efforts.

Thanks also goes out to Donnie Smith, Neil Ryan, and Scottie Ard for believing in me and helping to spread the passion for bikes into our future builders. I have only gotten as far as I have because of you.

A special thanks goes out to my father for his teachings and inspiration in something that is in our blood, and my mother for allowing me to grow up riding bikes. And the most important one goes to my wife and children for putting up with me being missing in action, as I often needed time away to focus on the book. I could not have done it without their love and support, Amy; you are the best wife ever!

Introduction

In this new age of bike building things have gotten extremely high tech. Huge fat tires and monster horse power engines seen on TV definitely influenced many new people to get into the bike riding and building craze. Although technological advancements have helped motorcycles become a more safe reliable mode of transport, it also seems to have transformed the cool simple look of a bike into some space ship contraption. I often wonder how much further the designs and ideas will be pushed when my boys are old enough to build their first bikes, and if they will make the decision to build something like Grandpa or Dad rides, or go with what the latest magazine says is cool.

Whenever I see that cool new part, design or invention come out, it doesn't take long to realize that although it may be the hottest new thing to get for your bike now, next year it will be probably laying on a swap meet table. The greatest thing about the old vintage style bikes is their no nonsense clean simple approach that has drawn people in for over 100 years. Less is definitely more and the bike scene has made a huge split down the middle on this subject. There are the flashy new school bikes and riders and then there are the clean simple old school bikes and riders. The new school rider seems to be the first to order that fancy new part to try and one up the other bikes like theirs at the shows, while the old school rider doesn't care much about that and sticks to simple timeless pieces that make the bike look like it could have been locked in a time capsule for 50 years. To me if you don't appreciate an antique bike, you definitely do not truly have bikes in your blood. Anyone who has bikes in their soul can not deny the history and beauty of how things were done by our forefathers.

This book is designed to show examples of some clean old-skool styled bikes. Some are true vintage antiques, while some are new technology bikes utilizing the time proven formula for the retro look. Whether you use use old parts or new, building a bike with this stance was cool a long time ago and will still be cool a long time from now.

If you have purchased this book and are about to embark on a new build, congrats and good luck. I know the bike will be something you can be proud of and after the trendy styles have died out your old skool ride will still be a head turner..

Chapter One

History and Background

Back In The Day

The term "old skool" has become one of the most popular phrases in the motorcycle riding, and building, community today. Old-skool "Choppers" and "Bobbers" have come back into the forefront of what's cool in the bike industry.

There is a huge group of riders who never got into the wide tire craze and always stayed true to their own vintage style. A lot of the new riders are looking for something besides fat-tire bikes, and want to go back to the basics of the custom

This 1955 Panhead owned by Gennaro is a true old-skool beauty. This magneto fired Pan is definitely a poster child for a cool, old-skool Bobber.

building style. Bikes with smaller tires and minimal rake and stretch are gaining in popularity fast. I spoke with Weyland from Solutions Machining, a true old skool builder, about his take on the term "old skool" and how it has been used in the bike community. "Hmmm... what does 'old skool' mean to me...? I gotta tell ya - right about now it means that I'm pretty tired of hearing 'old skool.' Ideally, it used to be used (or is supposed to be) used as a descriptive phrase that shows how something embodied certain aesthetic qualities, as well as personal embodiments, of the type of bike that was built in an earlier era. These days, though, there's been a watering down of its validity to the point where the term is being used incorrectly when simply referring to things like rigid frames and sprung seats."

MY GOAL

With that being said, the focus of this book is to help direct you in your quest for knowledge in building a bike the correct way. Cutting corners and making a bike unsafe is not considered a good way to achieve this style of bike. Please always make safety your number one priority in any bike building you do.

Father and son bonding at the Milwaukee Hard Tail party with our Panheads. That 1952 bobbed Pan has been my father's for over 38 years, he has had the old skool style his whole life, way before it was popular in the mainstream.

A vintage photo of my father on his 1952 Pan over 35 years ago. He had a love for the old Bobbers long before the life style was as accepted as it is today.

My wife and I on my father's cool stroked Shovelhead. This bike also has been in the family for over 20 years.

NEW AMERICAN HEROS

The whole industry was taken by storm with the first episode of American Chopper and the trend quickly spread to the Biker Build-off series. This helped millions appreciate custom motorcycles and the individuals who build them.

To me a true "old skool" bike is a bare bones bike that uses pre '84 parts. For me, stock bikes of these years qualify as well. For a true old skool Bobber, this is a bike of pre '84 parts which is built with the bare minimum, it has often been said, "if it doesn't make it go faster, or stop quicker, it gets taken off." The newest shiny gadgets and gizmos on the market are never used on these types of bikes. You'll rarely see a true old skool bike done in any type of "theme" except for functionality and nostalgia. The history behind the older bikes and their simplicity makes them all rolling museums, and to me the perfect work of art. I have never once pulled into a rally or event with my old Panhead without a bunch of people getting down on one knee to take a look at the old Pan in all its beauty, while they walk right past the new Choppers that seem to be so common.

DAD'S BIKES

I grew up around vintage bikes and through my father's influence learned to appreciate them for all they are.

My fathers bobbed Pan over 35 years ago. This bike has the old Bobber look that many are trying to achieve today.

Through the years of watching and learning about the things my father and his friends did to their bikes, I became dedicated to the style.

Point-fired distributors and magnetos are what I grew up on, working with Dad in his garage. Sometimes it was the repair of something broken, other times a modification made for performance or aesthetic reasons. In any case, I always appreciated their bare-bones, garage-building style. There weren't the big catalogs then that there are today. It was a time when if you wanted something cool you either saved your pennies for a long time for one piece, or you just went to the garage and built it yourself. My Dad's collection include a stroked 1974 Shovelhead Chopper, a stock 1964 police special sidecar Pan, a 1952 bobbed Pan, and a few other old Sportsters. This allowed me to get a good look at the different styles and find my own love for those bikes.

Whenever I'm at a rally like Sturgis or Daytona and I do stumble on an old Shovel, Pan or Knuck, I can spend a lot of time looking over the entire bike in fascination, checking out all that is still stock and noticing any modifications the owner may have made. These bikes were, and still are, the coolest, no matter what the current trend may be. They have survived the test of time and will outlast any fad that comes and goes in the industry.

A clean classic old Shovelhead. Bikes like this make for a great foundation to start your build. And for many this bike could easily be left just the way it is due to it's undeniable nostalgic beauty.

Big twins are not the only bikes that can be transformed into a cool old skool styled ride. This newer Sportster was built with some creativity and many hand made parts turning it into a unique looking ride.

9

Here is my bobbed 1967 TR6 Triumph, that again shows that v-twins are not the only bikes that can become great looking rides. This bike has a few old skool qualities to it. A Joe Hunt Mag, bolt on hardtail and bobbed fender give this bike a clean look.

WHAT'S A BOBBER?

Another huge item of discussion is the term "Bobber," what is a true Bobber and where did they come from? Bobbers can be found going back to the 1920's. Members of the Booze Fighters had many bobbed-style bikes, and in 1929 Harley Davidson came out with a factory Bobber with their D-series.

These bikes were stripped down factory customs with the elimination of the front brake and fender, as well as the cut-down bobbed rear fender. The early Bobbers were basically stock bikes with the hinged, rear half of the fender removed. Always popular among the racing riders, these old Harley's were often multi purpose vehicles for the owner. Not only a mode of normal transportation, but also their weekend race bike. Those who had traditional Harley's often would modify their bikes when they arrived at the competition site. They would pull up, and immediately start wrenching on the bike, stripping off all the excess weight in preparation for the race. Once the day's activities were completed they would reassemble the components to be street legal once again for the ride home. That's assuming they didn't crash badly during the race, which often happened.

For those who don't feel comfortable rebuilding

This Sucker Punch Sally bike blends old skool styling with new technology to give you a highly dependable retro-looking ride. This one utilizes a stock rake frame, no stretch, and 16 inch front and rear tires to achieve a great look.

old parts and using the vintage pieces, the old skool" look" can be achieved by using new aftermarket parts. These bikes generally include the bobbed rear fender and the elimination of any extra pieces and parts.

CHROME?

Back in the day, there weren't many chrome shops, and if there were, most bike owners didn't have the cash to have a lot of parts chrome plated. When building a Bobber, chrome and billet accessories are mostly eliminated to get that old style look. Turnsignals and extra lights are likewise tossed out. Flat black paint or flaked out retro-style paint gives these bikes that unique look. A look much like what a builder might have used back in 1940 or 1950.

Chrome is not the focal point on these bikes. Wrapped pipes, vintage parts that show some wear, and even flat black paint or powder coated parts give the bikes character. These bikes should, and are usually built to be ridden and not trailered to shows.

There is nothing more beautiful than a shiny restored old bike, but don't feel that beauty is from shine alone. Some of the coolest bikes I have ever seen were the dirtiest grungiest pieces of vintage iron. The kind of bike that you wish could talk and tell you its life story.

Another Sucker Punch creation that has the look of a vintage ride. The double white wall 16 inch tires and the turned down bars, with no front fender, give this bike an old-style attitude.

The stout, no-frills look of a stock frame and short front end give the Bobbers a compact look all their own.

11

Old skool Bobbers in their true form often did not have rake modifications in the frames, the rear fenders were cut or bobbed, and many other items were taken off the bike to decrease weight. Old skool Choppers on the other hand often incorporated the longer front end and frame modifications in the rake and stretch. Many of the first Choppers were stock rake and stretch frames that just used a longer front end, this created a bike with a very un-level frame and sat much higher in the front. If you come across any pictures from bike rallies in the '60s or '70s, you will see many bikes built like this. My father has owned the same 52' Panhead since before Vietnam, and it has seen the transition of all the different eras and styles. Before he went to 'Nam he had the stock Harley Springer front end on his stock Panhead frame set up in the Bobber style.

While he was in 'Nam, he ordered parts to make his Bobber a Chopper. He would even have my grandpa send him pictures holding the parts he ordered, to be sure they were the correct ones.

My grandfather holding a springer my Dad bought while in Vietnam. Pa would order parts by mail and then have gramps send pictures when they arrived to be sure he received the correct parts.

After 'Nam, my father tore down his Pan and added the new parts he ordered. The tall stance of the bike was common in those days for guys who added extended front ends and didn't change the frame rake.

After the military, he added the extended springer fork to his Panhead, but without changing the neck. The result is a bike that seems to be going uphill (note the nearby photo), like many of the other Harleys and Choppers of the period.

That was definitely old skool, if you couldn't afford a custom frame or the frame rake, you just scrapped together enough money for extended fork tubes or lengthened Springer, and that was it.

Today he has the bike set up with the stock-length fork, a set of dog bones and classic ape hangers, with the fat-bobs tanks, which brings it back to the Bobber style.

AFTERMARKET HELP

Today a new bike with the old-skool look can be built easily with the wide variety of aftermarket parts available to the builder looking for this style. Jammer Cycle Products, V-Twin, J&P vintage, as well as others all have vintage style aftermarket parts and equipment to help in achieving the vintage style. A popular frame rake for the old skool Bobber look would be 30-36 degrees with little or no stretch to the frame. This foundation allows for a tight compact bike that is quick and nimble. This is also the style of the late Indian Larry. Indian Larry, Paul Cox, and Keino have built a collection of the retro old skool styled bikes from old and new parts giving their bikes the look this book is trying to explain. They definitely brought old skool back to the forefront of cool, as was very apparent in Larry's victories in the Biker Build Off series. If you want to see great examples of old skool bikes built with new technology, check out their web site.

Another company that has really taken old skool to the next level is Sucker Punch Sally. Jeff and Don put together a working-man's special that allows the everyday garage builder a chance to build one of these cool retro-looking rides. I have personally used one of their rolling chassis kits, as Sucker Punch donated one of the frames to my high school shop class. We can verify that these frames are high quality and complete, so anyone can assemble one of their kits. There are old-skool builders, like Flyrite Choppers, and many others, who all supply what is needed for the bike you desire. The internet is a great tool to use in finding companies to compare products and to get build ideas.

For an old skool Chopper, there are many variations, and it is highly recommended you look at different frames and styles to find the one that fits you best. This book shows three different bike builds (Chapters Eight, Nine and Ten) that

A true old-skool Bobber owned by my father for almost 40 years. This bike is a head turner wherever it goes and does not need to be decked out in full chrome to be a cool ride.

The stock frame, flat fender and original springer front end show off the stout Bobber look these bikes possess. A Pan like this will never go out of style.

This SPS bike is a nice combination of retro styling with 21st century reliability.

The popularity of Bobbers can't be denied. Many of the display bikes at this year's Cincinnati trade show were in fact Bobbers - like this slick ride complete with modern Indian V-twin engine.

Old meets new. Another display bike, this one powered by a Twin Cam engine mated to a Evo-style 5-speed transmission.

mix new with old: a 1957 Panhead basket case, and two bikes composed of all new aftermarket parts incorporating some old skool flavor and design characteristics. The first school bike project is a board-track inspired Spartan frameworks frame and springer build, and the second is a Sucker Punch Sally bike built with a Spartan springer.

The goal of this book is to share some insights on my view of what old skool is, and what your options are if you decide to build a bike with this style in mind. As with anything else, there will be people who have different opinions and views about certain topics. All information in this book is based my personal experience and from talking with other builders. I started building bikes when I was a young kid. My first bike was a mini-bike powered by an old Briggs and Stratton engine. Now I am a high school shop teacher who has started a course devoted to building Choppers and Bobbers in class with the students. We try to build old skool bikes and want each one to be different, unique and original. Bikes that will not get lost in the crowd.

Every person you talk to may bring up different information or ideas on what should be used. I always recommend that you shop around, ask questions, and try to gather as

This Sucker Punch Sally Panhead was built with new parts, but looks like it came out of a 1950's calendar. The new technology utilized on a Panhead like this makes it a far superior choice for the beginner who is not ready to rebuild old, worn out parts.

A clean sleek drag inspired ride. This bike, built by Sucker Punch Sally, has a look that makes you want to get on it and do some burn outs!

The open belt and suicide shift are some of the most popular old skool touches to give a bike. Be aware of the safety concerns associated with riding bikes like this. Anyone without extensive motorcycle riding experience should think twice before attempting to run a bike like this.

much information, and as many design ideas, as possible before beginning your build. Using an approach to include all aspects and skill levels of builders, regardless if you have ridden for many years or are just getting started, this book will hopefully help to steer you in the right direction on your quest to create a vintage-looking ride.

The goal is not to show you how to do a true restoration of your bike but just to offer ideas on what might make for a cool, chopped, old skool Bobber style bike. There are many variations to old skool bikes but a few certain characteristics always are apparent on the Bobbers. Through pictures and step by step sequences you will see various options for the different pieces needed to build an old skool bike, and although some of the bikes pictured may not be exactly what you want they will offer design ideas that you can use or modify to fit your taste. There is nothing better than taking on the task of researching and exploring different bike styles, and components. The idea is to put together your own personal list of features that you want to incorporate into your new motorcycle. I would advise everyone to look around, ask questions, and don't rush into anything. GOOD LUCK!

My bobbed Panhead shortly after rebirth from barn rescued basket case. The entire bike was rattle can painted with flat black for the rat rod look.

This low slung creation (see Chapter Nine) utilizes all new aftermarket parts but borrowed some of the styling from an old board track racer. Anything is possible today with the wide variety of parts and accessories on the market.

This split-rocker Shovel has a super clean Bobber look. The elimination of exposed fender struts and the fender-mounted Sparto taillight add to the unique look.

Chapter Two

Bobber Frames

Buy One That's Safe and Legal

A big part of any bike build starts with the chassis. The frame is the foundation for how the bike will look. There are many options in original frames, aftermarket frames, vintage reproductions, custom Choppers, diggers, and anything you can dream up. Because of the large variety and options you really need to do your homework and become educated on frame style and design, before making a choice. Do not rush into the first frame you come across, and keep in mind the entire process,

This neat little Bobber rolling chassis kit from Kustomwerks is an inexpensive way to start on that next Bobber project.

and how you want the finished bike to look. If you do not look at the big picture and plan your build, the assembly will most definitely take more time and money to actually finish.

Old skool, retro Bobber-style bikes should utilize a frame with stock rake and stretch, meaning the dimensions an old Panhead, or Knucklehead, Harley-Davidson frame would have had as built at the factory. Many aftermarket frame manufacturers sell replica frames that match almost any vintage style. Whether you want a wishbone or straight-leg-rigid frame, or single-down-tube 45 frame, someone has what you need. One main criteria for an old skool build, in my opinion, is definitely a rigid frame. A swingarm takes away from the bare-bones, hard-core old skool look that was predominant before Harley-Davidson introduced the Duo-Glide in 1958. Can an old skool looking bike be created with a swing arm frame? Absolutely, but in my opinion rigid is the way to go.

A frame with little or no stretch and 30-36 degrees of rake, utilizing a 150 tire (at most) is the perfect foundation for an old skool looking ride. This gives the bike the compact, stout look apparent on all pictures seen of the vintage Bobbers. Although I have come across some builders who build cool old skool bikes with wider tires, it comes

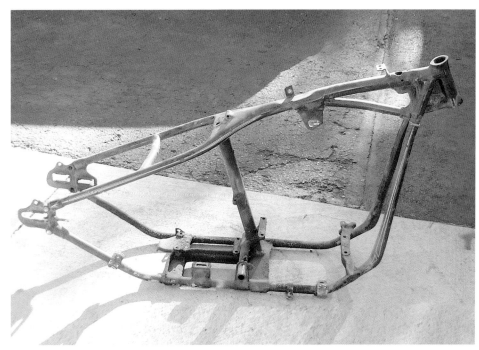

This barn find, straight-leg, rigid original Harley-Davidson frame was the victim of the Chopper era with many original pieces cut off or welded over. These frames are becoming more rare, especially un-cut ones, as many suffered changes to rake and stretch.

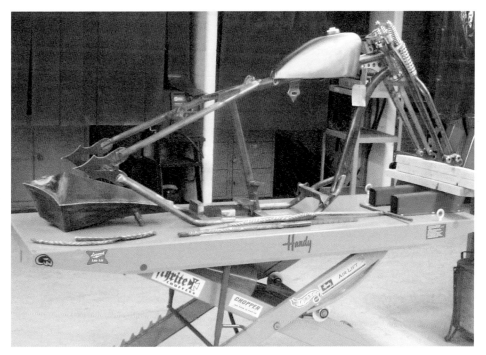

This frame has the stance that will go nicely with the old skool build. It has also has some custom axle plates and a Ford radius rod single down tube for a vintage look.

down to your personal preference on what tire to use and how the finished bike should look. If you're looking for more of an old-school fat tire chopper, Billy Lane is a great reference for styling tips on bikes of this type. If you want to keep more of the true vintage styling there are many websites that showcase pictures of Bobbers on the internet. By just typing in the keyword "Bobbers" you can find many, cool informative sites. One great way to help in deciding what to build is to collect pictures of different bikes with the look you want. These can be used to aid in your choice of parts and components when you order everything to build your own bike.

A no-rake, no-stretch, SPS frame with a Spartan 2 inch under riveted springer is a great combination for a unique retro styled ride.

CHOSE THE MOTOR

Before picking a frame, you have to decide which motor you plan to use. Shovels, Pans, and Evos will fit on the same motor mount points, but the Evolution sits higher than the Pan or Shovel, meaning you have be sure you have enough height in the backbone to accommodate the motor. If the frame needs to be modified to allow for the taller motor, measure and modify so the rocker covers don't hit the frame, and the seat post clears by about 3/4in. If you still have not decided on the exact motor make sure the frame you get is tall enough to accom-

More and more companies are offering Bobber-style rolling chassis kits. This assembly from Lee's Speed Shop is based on a Paughco frame with 30 degrees of rake, and a +2 inch reproduction springer. Rear fender is a vintage bobbed Knuck fender. Rear tires is 200/60X16, front is 3.50X18 inches.

modate any of the three choices you may pick. Also take into consideration the transmission you plan to use. Certain frames are manufactured specifically for certain transmissions, although you can get almost any transmission to work, it will make things go together smoother if you plan ahead.

IMPORTANCE OF A MOCK UP

Once you choose your frame and finally get it into your shop, mock-up can begin. At this stage, the frame needs all necessary tabs and brackets installed - before the bike is sent to paint. If you're lucky, all that you should have to do on most aftermarket frames, or stock originals, is add some tabs for custom exhaust. Depending on the gas tank, oil tank and rear fender you use, it may be necessary to add tank mounts or mounting brackets for the fender. Many aftermarket frames are available with the gas and oil tank, and their mounts, already installed.

Other additions may include some extras such as a remote oil filter kit, which can have a weld-on bracket to attach the filter assembly, or a side mount license plate bracket attached to the frame. If you are using a true, original frame these types of modifications are not recommended, as it will greatly decrease the value of the hard-to-find original. Many original frames are the victims of the Chopper era.

This original straight-leg Pan frame needs some work, but still holds a high value on the market today. Always inspect original frames carefully for any hidden damage, before the purchase.

Many original Harley-Davidson frames did not make it out of the Chopper era without some sort of modification. This one needed floorboard tabs, a tool box mount, and is still missing the side-car loops. The frame was also slightly bent and required some work to get it straight.

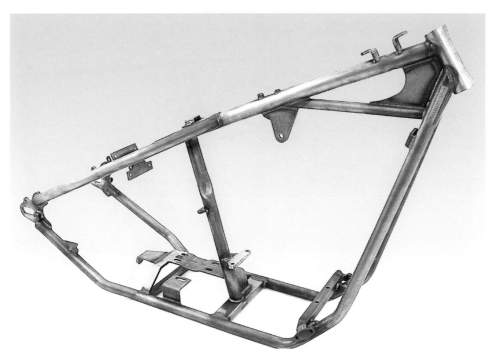

A wide variety of hardtail frames are available, from examples like this one from Kustomwerks with stretched downtubes, meant for a Evo or pre-Evo engine and 5-speed transmission...

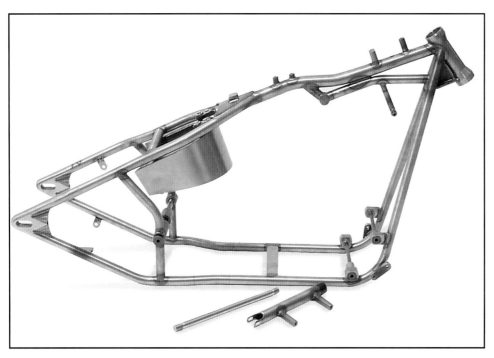

...to examples like this with conservative dimensions, designed for a Twin Cam B engine and transmission. Biker's Choice

Chopping often meant removal of tool box mounts, side car loops, neck locks, and floorboard tabs. Now, if you come across a true, original uncut frame it is worth a lot of money and to modify it from stock would be foolish! If you want to do that I recommend an aftermarket frame, or an original that's already been cut up.

Your frame options are: build one from scratch, buy an original, or buy a replica or aftermarket frame. The hardest of the three options would be to build your frame from scratch, which would require good welding skills and equipment, a frame jig, and the availability to bend tubing, and machine parts. This option should only be done by trained professionals to be sure the frame is fabricated safely and correctly.

Black Label Frame Works gave me the low down on how to correctly build a frame. To start, proper materials must be used to ensure a safe frame. Once the materials are on hand a high quality, accurate frame jig is a must to ensure that a straight functional frame will be created. Lastly, some superior welding skills are needed to guarantee the parts will be joined together correctly and that the welds will not break. If you do have access to the equipment and poses the skills to build a frame, I would recommend it. However, if you do not, find a qualified shop to do it for you. I highly recommend a shop like Black Label who can build a frame to your specifications.

RAKE AND TRAIL

When a custom built frame is created one of the most important parts of the build will be to incorporate proper rake and trail into the design. Rake is the angle in degrees the steering neck is angled from vertical. A rake of zero degrees would mean your neck is straight up and down. As the neck's angle is changed to a given degree, that measurement in degrees will be the rake. Most factory produced stock motorcycles have rakes from the high twenties to the mid thirties. These bikes are generally easy to maneuver and are stable at both low and high speed.

Trail is the distance between the front tire's contact patch and the point where the centerline of the bike's steering axis meets the ground (see the illustration). Motorcycles have positive trail. Like the caster angle of a car, positive trail provides the straight line stability that allows us to take our hands off the bars while going down the highway.

With a custom bike, the rake is often changed or exaggerated to get a certain look, but you have to keep in mind that more rake generally gives you more trail. While you do need some

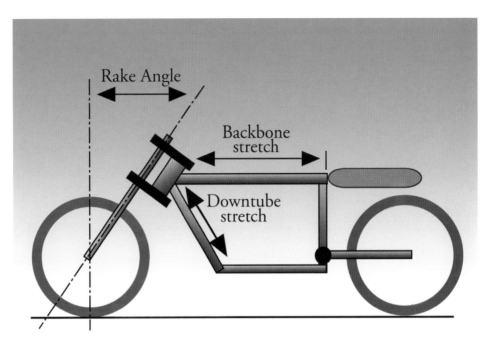

We now have two kinds of stretch, in the top tube and the downtubes. On the street, people talk about a certain frame as having, "a 38 degree neck that's "3 ahead and 4 up."

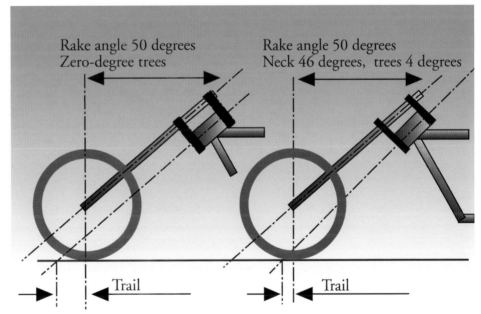

Many experienced Chopper builders get part of their total rake from the trees, as a way to reduce the trail and thus some of the heavyness that comes with extreme rake angles.

You can measure trail with a tool like that shown, which is nothing more than a piece of aluminum tubing that slides over an aluminum rod. The rod is attached to the bike through a short cross-piece bolted to the bottom triple tree - which means it's aligned with the centerline of the neck.

Here you can see how the distance between the tip of the tool and the centerline of the axle gives the trail dimension.

positive trail for stability, you can also have too much of a good thing.

MEASURE TRAIL

When designing a bike, the safe amount of trail is generally in the four to six inch range. This can and must be accomplished on any set up regardless of your rake angle. There are exceptions that have been demonstrated in the bike building industry, but for a safe start stick to these numbers. To correctly measure your trail, set your bike in the upright position with the handlebars straight. Measure straight down from the center of the front axle to the floor and place a mark. Next, use a straight edge or tape and follow the centerline of steering neck all the way to the floor. Place a mark on the floor where the line hits the ground.

Measure the distance between the two marks and you have your trail (note the nearby photos). If it is 4 inches or very close to it you are in the so-called safe zone. One thing to remember is to allow for the drop in height of your frame when you are sitting on it, if it has rear suspension. This can be done by sitting on the bike while someone else takes the measurements, or by doing all your calculations at ride height.

TOO MUCH OR TOO LITTLE

Some sport bikes, Buells for example, have as little as three and a half inches of trail, which makes for a very nimble bike.

Most experienced builders, and most Harley-Davidsons, stay in the four to six inch zone. If you have too much trail, a measurement over six inches, the bike may be heavy to turn at speed and want to "flop" at low speeds. Most typical Bobber-type frames with conservative rake angles of 28 to 32 degrees will net you trail figures in the zone mentioned above, but it's always a good idea to check (before you finish the bike). There are a variety of trail calculators on the web, including one at RB Cycles (rbracing-rsr.com/rakeandtrail), and another inside the cover of your Drag Specialties catalog.

If you find after getting your bike all together that the rake or trail is not in the recommended zone there are a few things that can be done to fix this. There are raked triple trees that can be used on glide style front ends to reduce trail. Raked trees reduce trail, which is why it's a bad idea to put raked trees on stock frames (you end up without enough positive trail) and why Chopper builders often used raked trees when the frame has a rake angle of 38 or more degrees. Raked neck cups are now being sold as well, to modify the angle. If a Springer front end is being used modified rockers can be created to help with these problems as well. Some

Described as the "ultimate in retro cool" this rolling chassis kit from Jammer is based on a "stripped '48 Panhead," complete with a straight-leg style frame, with 33 degrees of rake and an extra 2 inches of stretch in the downtubes. Accepts nearly any Pre T-C engine. Comes with Fat Bob tanks, 40 spoke wheels.

A finished bike based on the rolling chassis kit seen above. Front tire measures 21 inches, rear is a 130X16. Brakes from GMA. Jammer

A donor Sportster and a hardtail frame can be combined to build a very inexpensive Bobber. The frame shown here comes with an extra 5 degrees of rake and no stretch in either the top tube or downtubes. Accepts Evo Sporty engines up to 2001. Biker's Choice.

This swingarm frame resembles the FX factory frames (pre-Evo) used for FL and Super Glide bikes. Uses typical factory dimensions, including rake. Biker's Choice

Springer manufacturers, like Redneck Engineering, will tailor make your Springer to incorporate the right trail figure if you give them the rake and frame dimensions before ordering the fork assembly.

To be safe always get a qualified motorcycle mechanic to check your trail and help correct any problem, this is an area where it's definitely better to be safe than sorry.

BACK TO THE FRAME

If you choose to use an original frame you may even be lucky enough to get a complete running bike that you can slowly work on, making the modifications while still being able to ride. This is a great option if you are not in a rush to complete the entire project in a short time frame, and it still allows for some riding between modifications. This also helps avoid the title issues that often come with building from swap meet parts. Be aware when buying a used frame, there may be hidden problems. Any frame that is molded with filler could possibly be hiding imperfections and hazards. Always ask to see the frame in a sand blasted bare metal finish before purchasing, and go over the entire frame looking for any previous repairs or damages. Although the majority of the sellers out there are most likely honest there are a few who may be looking to pull the wool over your eyes.

Because of this it is

hard to be 100% sure you are getting what is being advertised, unless you can carefully examine the frame before the purchase. Use extra caution when you find frames with filler, primer, or freshly painted surfaces. This often is the work of someone trying to cover up problems.

With an original frame, you also need to be sure it is the correct one for the motor you will use. Generally, Knuckleheads and Flatheads can be put in the same frames with little modifications, these frames only really differ in the motor mount area of the frame. If you were to try and fit a Pan, Shovel or Evolution in these frames, more extensive frame modifications would be needed to create more space in the top tube and seat post, or the motor will hit in those areas.

Shovelhead frames have more clearance than the Flat and Knucklehead frames. An Evolution motor, if used in one of these frames, will usually force you to make modifications to create enough clearance.

An aftermarket frame is your third option. This means you are starting from scratch and will have to keep records of all your purchases. These receipts will be used when you make the trip to the DMV for inspection and titling. This option does make it easy to pick out the exact rake and stretch you want to be sure the bike will have the fin-

From Paughco comes this "stock style rigid frame" with wishbone downtubes, Fat Bob mounts, and stock rake and stretch dimensions. Works best with Pan or Shovel engines, and chain drive to the rear wheel. Biker's Choice

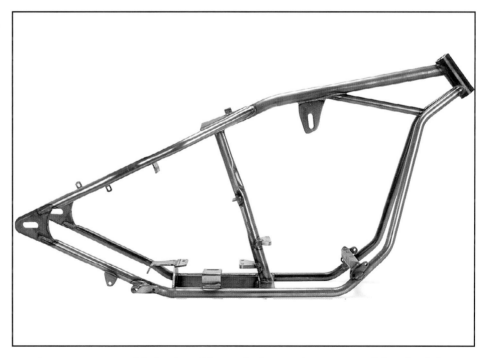

Perhaps not a true old skool, Bobber style frame, this goose-neck hardtail frame from Santee is available with up to 38 degrees of rake and a rear section wide enough for a 230 tire with belt drive. Jammer

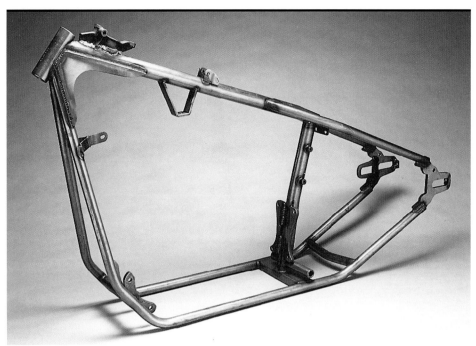

Another chance to make good use of that old Sporty in the garage, this Santee frame is designed to accept an Iron-head engine and transmission. Rake is 33 degrees, downtubes are stretched 2-1/2 inches. Tank mounts on the top tube for early style Fat Bob tanks. Jammer

More hardtail options. This straight-leg frame from Santee will accept Evo and pre-Evo engines, with 5-speed tranny. Comes with or without mounts for early style Fat Bob tanks.

ished stance you want. Be sure to research the various manufacturers and ask questions. The frame is one of the most important pieces of your bike-to-be, and you would not want to start off with an unsafe or incorrectly built frame. A poor decision here will come back to haunt you in the long run. There are many companies that offer customer feedback and limitless tech support and help, such as Sucker Punch Sally's. A company like SPS has a great reputation for quality and it is easy to track down happy customers to ask about their building experience, and to get recommendations regarding the company. With anything you purchase, always remember, "You get what you pay for." Cutting corners, buying a cheap frame, will only cause problems in the long run. If you truly want to build the bike of your dreams and have it be a safe and reliable bike, do your research and make well-informed quality purchases. If you buy a cheap frame from a company that does not have credibility, or back up their product, you may very well be scrapping the frame down the road only to have to purchase a new one in it's place. A frame made cheaply can be prone to cracking if the wrong materials and processes were used in it's assembly. There are other potential problems as well, like incorrect alignment and misplaced mounts that will cause many assembly headaches. If the motor mounts or transmission mounts are mis-aligned the bike will not go together properly! Always visit the frame manufacturer if possible to inspect their production facility and get a feel as to whether or not they are a fly-by-night company.

There are many new frame builders that are here today and gone tomorrow. You would hate to hand over a large lump of your hard earned cash to find out down the road they went under and can no longer be contacted. The good manufacturers are proud of their companies and take pride in what they do. They will be able to show you samples, testimonials and proof that they have been doing it right since the beginning and will be doing it right long after your purchase. Use common sense and good judgment with any company you choose, there are many great small operations creating quality frames, such as Spartan Frameworks. George is a one-man fabricator who takes great pride in his unique, one-of-a-kind, hand-fabricated creations. He also has strict quality control and will only allow top quality frames to leave his shop. He knows that his best advertisement is happy customers, and through continuous hard work and top notch work he has built some of the coolest frames and front ends on the market today.

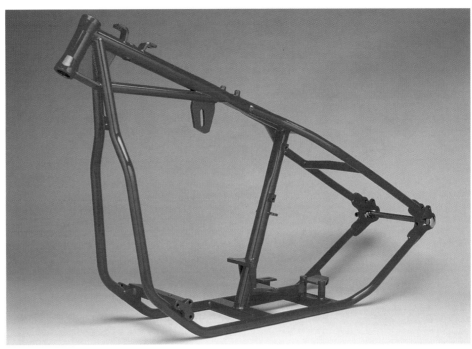

Remember, the frame will determine the overall look of your new bike. In this case, the look will be traditional, with wishbone downtubes, no extra stretch, 30 degree rake, Fat Bob tanks (later style), and 4-speed transmission with chain final drive. Custom Chrome

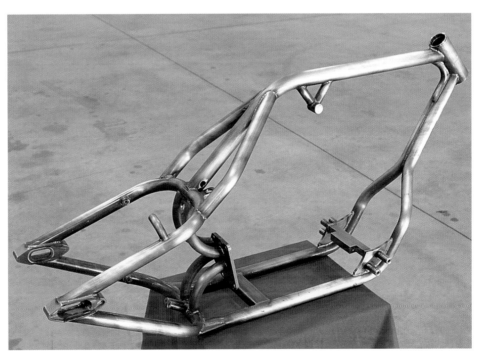

For a more modern twist on the hardtail theme, consider this frame from Redneck Engineering, designed to accept the drivetrain from a Buell or Sportster.

Whether it's a soft-tail or hardtail frame, quality depends on good material, (either mild steel or chrome moly) a good, accurate frame jig, good fitment between individual pieces, and good welders. Note the size of the table and fixtures that make up this Rolling Thunder frame fixture. C. Maida

At Rolling Thunder they use a special tool to cut a perfect concave notch in the tube...
C. Maida

To make things even easier many companies now offer complete rolling chassis where you can quickly choose the rake and stretch to match the style you want to build. This eliminates any problems you may have buying the correct components that will work with your chassis. All the parts are put together as a kit often with options that can be added, and you get it all delivered to your door.

Even complete running bikes can be purchased through companies at a very reasonable price. The best advice is to always shop around and determine if you have the know-how to build a bike from scratch, or if you should buy a kit bike, or even a complete running bike.

No matter which route you choose, keep in mind you will eventually have to either transfer or apply for, a new title for the bike. Don't get caught with improper paperwork or botched numbers, you can be denied a title and could lose the bike! Federal law states that all motor vehicles must be titled and must have a 17-digit Vehicle Identification Number (VIN). Since 1981, the title must match the frame numbers to be legal. Harley's that are pre 1969 did not have numbers on the frames so the title matched the engine only. Be aware that if you buy an existing bike to modify, and you do not have the previous owner's title for the bike, it will be much more difficult to make legal.

More information on the process of transferring a title can be found here: www.dmv.org/title-transfers.php. On an aftermarket frame you will need the Manufacturers Statement of Origin (MS0) to show proof of where the frame was built. Since every state can be different in their rules regarding titling a vehicle it is strongly recommended to first check with your state's Department of Motor Vehicles before purchasing anything. Determine what you need to make the bike legal before turning over your cash. A good rule of thumb is to document everything and save all receipts for every piece of the bike. With any purchase, be aware that the State's main goal is to eliminate the use of stolen parts, so buying swap-meet parts can be a big problem. Although many swap meets offer good deals on parts that you can use on your project, parts with botched numbers, no titles, or other unknowns may draw a big red flag at the DMV. Always err to the safe side, and if at all possible, buy new parts with proper MSOs. This will definitely aid in proving that the bike is not stolen and was built from legit parts.

The DMV web site (www.dmv.org/) will have a link for each state, and that site should have either a link that will give you information on the process and requirements for titling a bike, or a phone number to call to get the information.

...you could do the same thing by hand with a small grinder. The important thing is that the two pieces fit together nice and tight before the welding begins. A tight fit means the welds are stronger and neater, as there is no need to fill gaps. This also means less heat, which means less warpage. C. Maida

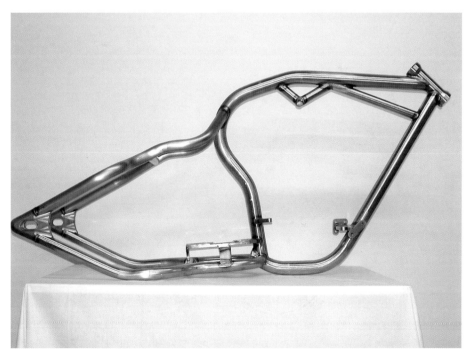

The end result is a hardtail Big-Twin frame that's straight and strong, with engine and transmission mounts that line up perfectly during assembly. C. Maida

31

Chapter Three

Chassis Components

Forks, Wheels & Rims

There are three types of fork assemblies you can choose from for your build. The Telescopic or Hydraulic fork, the Springer fork, and the Girder. Each of the three are unique in their own way, and will drastically change the appearance and the ride of your bike. As with anything else, you will hear pros and cons from different people, so the best way to decide which front

This Redneck bobber kit comes with their own Springer fork assembly, a 21 inch spoked rim and disc brakes.

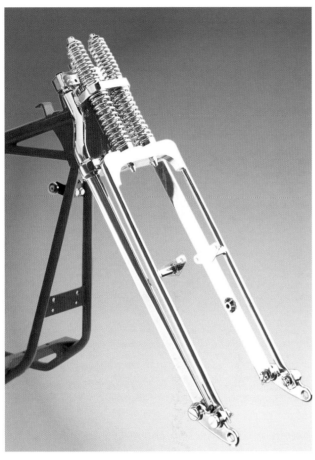

From Custom Chrome comes this complete Springer fork assembly, available 2 inches under to 6 inches over.

end is the right one for you is through proper planning and research.

After talking with Weyland from Solutions Machining and Welding about the three front-end styles, we came to this conclusion: all three are valid suspension systems for the Average Joe to consider, but Average Joe needs to be aware that Springers and Girders can cost considerably more than a typical hydraulic fork. In the performance to economics ratio, Hydros win hands down, any time. They've been being mass produced the world over for years, and are very inexpensive to manufacture, while offering good handling characteristics. They also are easily modified for length. To me, though, Springers and Girders are the epitome of Chopperdom. They're open mechanical-ness speaks to the heart of man. Technically, Springers and Girders

have many variations in form. There are leading link front ends, trailing link front ends, conventional Springers, inverted Springers, and Girders ranging from traditional and conventional, all the way through wildly experimental.

Springers and Girders have always been my personal favorites, based solely on the fact that I like the mechanical look of things, and there's little more mechanical than a well executed Girder or Springer. On a personal note, I'm a huge fan of Girders, speaking from a technical standpoint, due to their versatility and end user adjustability. Possibly my favorite Girder of all time (based on technical aspects) is John Britton's Girder used on his V1000. Infinitely adjustable for geometry, it could be used to create an "anti-dive" front suspension. For aesthetics, I doubt anyone will ever top Paul Cox's Girder on his Berserker Panhead, pure poetry in motion.

Because it's a Donnie Smith design, you know this Girder combines function with traditional form. Jammer

The Girder front end is the least used of the three choices and really has a unique vintage look. The girder front end has origins spanning almost 100 years, and are rated by many who have used them as being the most responsive, well handling front ends out there. Girders allow for great adaptability in frame configurations, and can be created to handle a broad spectrum of rake and stretch dimensions. Girders also are popular for their

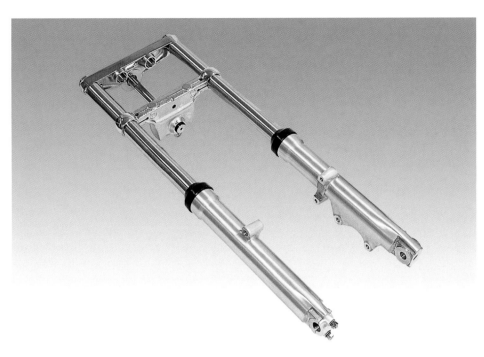

This complete 41mm fork assembly is available in a variety of lengths, set up to run disc brakes on one side. Kustomwerks

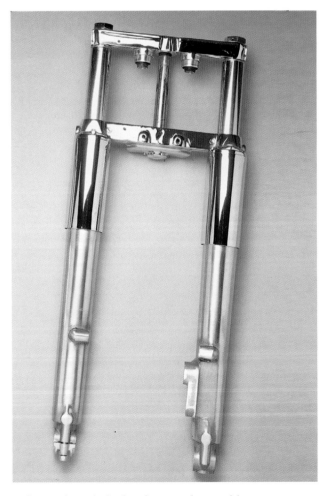

This early-style hydro front end assembly comes set up for either left or right side drum brake, or disc. Jammer

excellent braking characteristics and when set up properly offer one of the best rides out there. Custom Chrome still sells the Donnie Smith signature series Girders, otherwise you're going to need to check out swap meets, or custom builders who may fabricate one for you.

Weyland from Solutions Machining and Welding creates some of the most beefy and durable girders I have ever seen. Although you do not see the market flooded with aftermarket versions today, when you do see a bike with a girder it definitely stands out.

Second on the list for front ends being used are the Springers. Springers have seen action for over 80 years and have really boomed in recent years. Many aftermarket manufacturers are now offering a variety of Springer front ends. Springers are readily available and can be picked up at a reasonable price. The antique Harley-Davidson Springers definitely don't come cheap, but a chrome aftermarket example can be had for as little as $500.00. As with anything else, always check the quality of the product before laying down your hard earned cash. There are crooks out there selling unsafe garbage Springers that wouldn't be fit for a mini bike. I have seen some of the best and worst Springers at swap meets. Please do your research before trusting your life with one.

Springers are often thought of as unstable, rough riding, inefficient front ends. Actually, if well made, they can be set up to ride and handle nicely. This is where you really need to talk to the different manufacturers who've been building the front

This quality custom girder built by Black Label Frameworks is mated to one of their hand-crafted frames. Always be sure to choose a reputable company for your frame or front end, safety should always be the number one priority.

Wheels with tapered bearings require that you set the end play, (though with these traditional wheels the end play is already set) and pack the wheel bearings. Available in 16 and 21 inch diameters with chrome or stainless spokes. Jammer

ends for years and have tested them in many different situations. Let them know the specs of your frame, and work with them to create a functional work of art for your bike. George Counes, of Spartan Frameworks, creates some very high quality custom Springers. George said, "Springers are my personal favorites, you can feel the road through them. Plus they look cool with the mechanical aspect, you can watch them move. I think

This original offset springer was poorly cut and lengthened. If you use a fork that has been altered, be sure it was done properly and is in good condition.

Springers handle fine for every day hauling ass around town, and I do 90 miles per hour on the freeway without any problems. The "pogo" effect you may have heard of can be caused by poor rocker design, worn out springs, no inner springs, or under-sized springs. I have been running Springers on my personal bikes for 20 years, all hardtails and all short, and have never had a problem with 'pogo.' If you like Springers, put one on your bike, you'll like it."

The nearby photos show an example of an original offset Harley Springer that had been cut and extended by someone back in the Chopper days. We decided to bring this front end back to life at its original length. To start the transformation we acquired a second set of original legs that had the stem cut out with a torch, this offered a great donor set of legs. The problem with these is that over the years water had gotten into the legs (they were stored outside). During the winter the water froze, which put pressure on the legs and caused cracks and swelling. The damage was apparent right away. After we cut the legs off, we were able to examine the extent

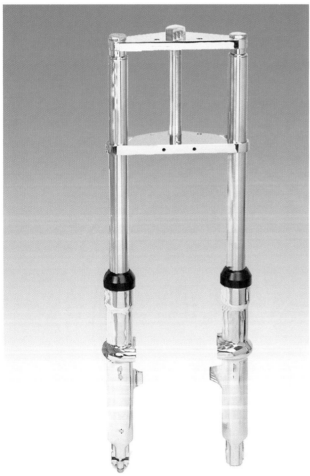

Similar to OEM fork assemblies from the late '70s and early '80, these forks accept dual early-style calipers. Jammer

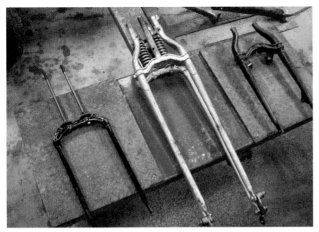

The lengthened offset springer in the middle, with the donor rear legs on the right, and a new set of stock length front legs on the left.

The legs aligned with the slugs inside and the rosettes welded in. The final welding can now begin. Always be sure to keep everything in proper alignment.

The rear legs were cut off at a 30 degree angle with as much of the original stock leg left as possible.

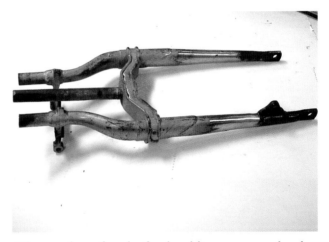

The rear legs after the final welding was completed, and all welds smoothed out with a 6x48 belt sander.

Steel slugs were made from chrome moly to be inserted at the point where the two leg sections will be joined for added strength. The slugs are a must when doing repairs of this type.

The finished offset springer brought back to stock length.

As we said, wheels come with either modern sealed bearings or more traditional tapered bearings. If your wheels have tapered bearings you must get the center spacer and shims needed to set the end play. These kits shown here fit a variety of early wheels and include both new bearings and seals. Jammer

When setting up new wheels in the frame, you will no doubt need wheel spacers. These brass spacers can be cut to the correct dimension, and add a nice early-skool feel to that Bobber project. Jammer

of the damage. We decided the part of the legs we needed was still in good enough shape to use, so we moved forward with the repair. After the legs were cut off of both forks, we created an inner slug that would be welded in at the joint where the leg repair was being made, for added strength and rigidity. We very carefully lined up the two sections to ensure proper placement when they were welded together. Both sets of the legs were drilled for rosettes. These are weld points that help to keep the pieces aligned and add strength to the welded joint. After the inner sleeves were inserted and the front end was aligned, the welding could begin. First the rosettes were welded up on the outside of the Springer. After they were filled in, the legs were rechecked for proper straight alignment. Once the alignment was checked the inside rosettes were welded up. The legs were again checked and after everything checked out to be straight, the rest of the seams were TIG welded. After the front end was completely welded, the welds were then ground smooth to hide the repair section.

Everything was then re-assembled and we had ourselves a nice antique Springer to use on the Panhead project.

The last of the three, and the most widely used, is the hydraulic fork. These front ends are readily available anywhere you go and are used for their comfortable ride and reliability. Companies like Harley-Davidson started using the Hydraulic fork almost 60 years ago on the 1949 Hydra-Glide Panhead. This front end was noticeable not only for its big telescoping forks but also for the increase in comfort and handling on the road. With the bigger front end there was an allowance for bigger front brakes, which also increased the bike's stopping power and safety. The hydraulic front end works through springs and hydraulic fluid to give a smooth comfortable ride that has a wide range of travel to eat up those big bumps you may encounter. Hydraulic front ends are the most common style seen at bike shows and swap meets, and can be easily purchased in any length to fit your needs.

Whichever style front end you pick, always ask the professionals for a second opinion and choose carefully. Be sure to take proper measure-

Designed by Chica, these retro Invader wheels come in 21 and 16 inch diameters. Rear wheels come with single or dual flanges. Jammer

There weren't chrome shops on every corner, back in the day. And if there were, the plating process was expensive. Thus, the original Bobbers didn't carry much chrome. You can duplicate that early look by disassembling and powder coating your rims and hubs, or buying them already coated in red or black from Jammer.

The classic styling of the Avon Speed master is a high-quality, new-technology tire with the retro look.

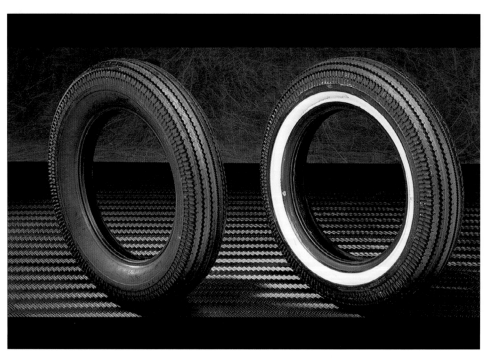

Fortunately for modern builders you can find a wide variety of aftermarket, retro styled tires on the market today. Always choose quality.

ments when ordering your frame to be sure that the new front end will leave your bike sitting level when it is installed on a fully assembled bike.

WHEELS AND TIRES

Choosing the correct wheel and tire combination can really give your bike that old skool vintage look. Ribbed speed grip or Goodyear style tires, with or without whitewalls, have always been a trademark and have made a huge comeback in the old skool style bike building scene. Many of the major tire companies have designed tires to replicate the old-skool look with the reliability of new tire technology.

There are Firestone, Goodyear, and Speed Grip tires being manufactured by Coker, Shinko, H-D, and Avon as well as some others. These tires give the old hill climber or bobbed racer look to the bike. Looking at vintage pictures these tires really gave the bike that extra something needed to achieve a unique style. Be sure you match your tires and wheels according to manufacturers specifications.

Rims for the old skool Bobber must be spoked, with the exception of the invader wheel which was used on many

These OEM style tires from Dunlop come in stock sizes with standard tread patterns. Biker's Choice

Whether you run a 19 inch front rim, or a 16 inch painted or chrome plated, the choice is yours and should be made in concert with all the other parts on the bike and your overall goal for the machine.

Make it fun, make it safe and make it your own.

Choppers in the 70s. Sixteen inch rear rims, with a width of 3.00 or 4.00, work great for the vintage look matched with a 21x 1.85 inch front wheel or the same 16-inch front. The new billet rims just don't have a place with the retro-style bike. A 40 spoke 16x3 inch rear and 21 inch front is the combination that was used on my '57 Panhead and the class project bike. This is a popular combination for the classic old-skool look. The vintage star hub can be found at swap meets, online or through aftermarket companies such as Jammer Cycle Products. For the hard core old-skool look, the spool front hub style wheel (which does not use a front brake) gives any bike that bare bones, super clean look.

Builder beware. It is not recommended that any bike be ridden without a front brake! The front brake gives you the majority of your quick stopping power if someone cuts you off. If you eliminate the front brake, you are taking away a great deal of stopping power and making the bike more dangerous to ride.

Lock in that old-skool-kool with wide whites from Avon. The "Gangster" model is available in only one, 90H16, size. Biker's Choice

Chapter Four

Brakes

Drum or Disc, Ya Gotta Have 'Em

Brakes are a very crucial part of any bike. Without good stopping power your chances of an accident are greatly increased. Riding a motorcycle can be a dangerous feat in itself, but add in a limited ability to stop when that Buick pulls out in front of you and you're playing Russian roulette! The old drum-style brakes are definitely a conversation piece at bike shows, and will draw some attention, but if you want true, reliable stopping power disk brakes are the

Seen at the Klock Werks shop, this new-school Bobber uses a two-piston caliper from PM. The small caliper provides good stopping power without the bulk of a big four-piston caliper.

way to go. This is especially true if you do not run a front brake. When building an old-skool Bobber the most retro look will be drum brakes, and possibly even no front brake. Now take it into consideration the fact that being cool does not mean reliable stopping power.

The old drum brakes definitely have a unique vintage look but are not as safe, or reliable, as the disc brake system. Any bike, even stock ones set up for mechanical brakes, can be modified to use a hydraulic disc braking set up.

Disc brakes are considered more reliable and provide a much better braking system than a drum. If you do want to run a mechanical drum brake and your frame does not have the cross tube, be ready for some welding and fabrication to get one installed and lined up correctly. If you want the look, drum is the way to go, if you want the safety factor, then run disc brakes. The choice is up to you and remember to take in consideration your riding terrain, traffic congestion and your riding ability when choosing your brakes. If you're running in a big city with lots of traffic and hills, I would highly recommend a disc brake system on both ends. At least put a disc on the bike's front end.

Dress up that Bobber with a chrome brake drum/sprocket, available for most mechanical and hydraulic brakes from '37 to '78, including many Sportsters. Jammer

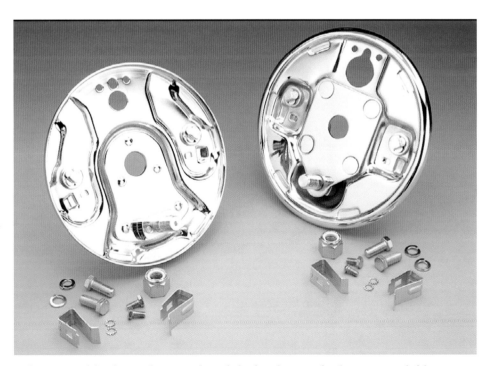

The original backing plates used with hydraulic rear brakes are available new, with chrome plating, in two models that cover the years '58 through '62, and '63 through '72. Jammer

PHYSICS OF BRAKES

Brakes work through the simple concept of pressure being applied to a drum or rotor. When you apply the brake, the brake pads exert pressure either outward to the drum or inward onto the rotor. The harder the brake pedal is pressed, the more pressure is exerted, which increases the stopping power.

When the pads contact the rotor, the components get hot. It's what brakes do, convert moving energy to heat. Bigger components are generally better able to handle that heat. You might think that each wheel has half of the potential stopping power, but as you stop the weight shifts to the front wheel, so the front wheel has way more than 50% of the potential stopping power.

DISC VS DRUM

Drum brakes were used on Harley-Davidsons from 1937 through 1972. Drum brakes work with either a mechanical or hydraulic set up. Although the brake changed through the years from the mechanical style to the juice brake, they never did get as good as a disc system. The mechanical-style drum brake utilizes a mechanical linkage to transmit the pedal's movement into movement at the brake shoes, forcing them apart and against the rotating drum. With juice rear brakes, pressure in the master cylinder forces fluid through the lines and into a wheel cylinder. Pressure in the wheel cylinder forces the shoes apart.

Drum brake systems have a few flaws in the

Everybody wants unobtrusive front brakes that still have good stopping power. The twin goals are accomplished here with a single two-piston caliper and small diameter rotor. PM

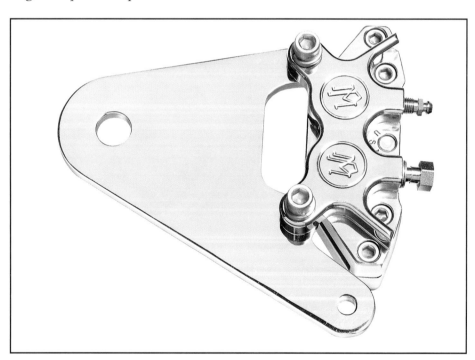

The simple caliper mount can be used with many rear brake applications. Includes the lower tab which can be used to anchor the mount to the frame through a short linkage. PM

design, that were eliminated in the disc brake system. Drums are typically very large, bulky, heavy pieces to have on a bike. The bigger the drum the more braking surface, but you must keep in consideration the extra weight the system will add to your bike. There are mini drum systems available but, in my experience and through talking with others, they are pretty much only good for holding the bike still at a stop light. Their rolling stopping power is inadequate to say the least. Add to that the fact that any grease, dirt, grim etc. that gets into the drum cannot escape - and there goes more of the crucial stopping power.

With the exception of some Mickey Mouse, mini-disc brakes, all real disc brake systems are hydraulic, and offer more braking power for a given amount of weight than a drum brake. Disc brake designs are also self-cleaning (dirt and debris are thrown to the outside) and they cool better than drum brakes do. In the end a disc brake is a better brake than a drum, and the better choice, especially for the front wheel.

This radial-style rotor from Hallcraft is a good match for spoked wheels, and fits most standard front and rear hubs. Biker's Choice

JUICE DISC BRAKES

Hydraulic disc brakes use brake fluid to transfer power from the master cylinder to the caliper and eventually the brake pads. Brake fluid (or any fluid) can't be compressed, so the full power of a lever pull is transferred to the caliper pistons. You don't want any air in the lines, because air can be compressed, which leads to a soft brake pedal or lever.

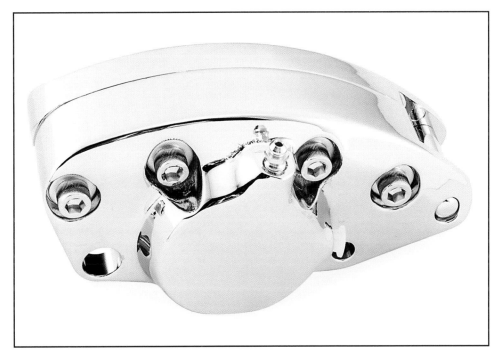

If you need that certain period-correct look, the "banana" calipers (used from '73 to '84 on various models) are available brand new, chrome plated and with new pads. Biker's Choice

Old wheel and master cylinders can be honed out and rebuilt with kits that include new cups and springs (as long as the bore is not pitted). Follow the procedure from any good Harley, or automotive, service manual, and wash the parts with clean brake fluid, not solvent. Biker's Choice

If the cylinder bore is pitted, or you're in doubt about the rebuilding process, just buy complete new replacement components like this new wheel cylinder for factory rear brakes. Biker's Choice

Hydraulic Ratios

The master cylinder you use needs to be matched to the caliper (or wheel cylinder), in the sense that the hydraulic ratios need to be considered. The hydraulic pressure leaving the master cylinder is determined by the formula: pressure = force/area. Ten pounds of force on a piston with one square inch of area gives you 10 psi in the lines and 10 psi acting on the caliper pistons. Obviously a smaller piston will net you more pressure (for a given amount of force) but at the expense of total volume displaced.

At the caliper end of the line a rearranged version of the same relationship is in effect. That is, force = pressure X area. So a caliper with big and/or multiple pistons will give you more force for a given amount of pressure. Again, more pistons give you more force but they also require a larger volume of fluid to be displaced by the master cylinder.

What this means in the long run is that you can't just grab a master cylinder from the used parts bin in your buddy's garage and match it up to a caliper you bought at a swap meet. If you have twin, four-piston calipers on the front of your Bobber (not likely), a master cylinder with a 3/4 inch piston is a better choice than one with a 5/8 inch piston.

If you're buying new parts, ask the salesperson or manufacturer for a recommendation. Too small a master cylinder piston will give you more pressure and less volume. Too big a piston will have the opposite effect. Your goal is to achieve balance between the master cylinder and caliper.

Before declaring success with the brakes, you have to bleed all the air out of the system, both front and rear. You can either do this by the tried, true, and tedious method, or with one of the many bleeding aids sold by the motorcycle aftermarket. The tedious method involves first bleeding the master cylinder with short strokes until no more bubbles appear in the reservoir. Next, you want to do two or three full strokes, hold the lever in the applied position (after the last stroke) and open the bleeder. A blast of air and fluid will escape. Now close the bleeder and repeat the process until no more air or fluid/air mixture escapes the bleeder.

The bleeding aids are all pumps of one sort or another. Some suck the fluid from the reservoir to and through the bleeder, while others add fluid at the bleeder and pump the system full.

Motorcycles, no matter how cool they are, are only good if they're usable. This means they need to start and run without hassle, and they should stop quickly when the truck pulls out in front of you. Unless it's truly a show bike, put some brakes on the front wheel, the wheel with more than half the potential stopping power in a panic situation.

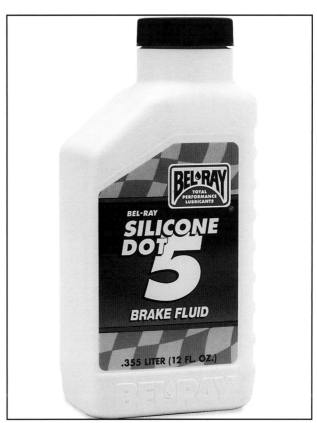

In about 1980, H-D switched to silicone (DOT 5) brake fluid. It's "better" in the sense that it doesn't absorb moisture, or attack paint. Be careful not to mix the 2 types of fluid.

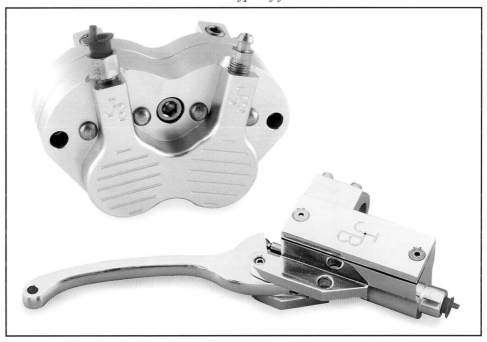

Front master cylinders range in piston size from about 9/16 to 3/4 inch diameter. Be sure the size matches the caliper(s). Also, drum-brake rear master cylinders use a residual pressure valve and should not be used with disc brakes. Biker's Choice

Chapter Five

Engines

Real Panheads are Great, but Expensive to Repair

To build a true vintage, old-skool looking Big Twin bike, a 45, Shovel, Panhead, or Knucklehead would be the first choice. Since this is not an easy option for many, and the fact that they are becoming harder to find and much more expensive to pick up, there are alternatives. The old-skool look can be achieved if you're using an Evolution or newer style motor from Harley or one of the many aftermarket motor manufacturers, as long as the rest of the bike follows the form and function of

RevTech (aka Custom Chrome) makes their own line of Evo-style engines in displacements up to 110 cubic inches. Custom Chrome

the vintage style. Many aftermarket motor manufacturers are also selling new motors with the Pan and Knucklehead look. S&S even has a new generator Shovel on the market! If you're not a hardcore mechanic and do not want the hassle of having to work on an old vintage motor, an aftermarket motor is definitely the choice. The top choices of the aftermarket are definitely one of the retro styled motors.

Pans were, for years, the quintessential Chopper motor. As they (and we) get older, we're seeing more and more Shovels being used for the basis of many chops and customs. I am sure, as time goes on we will see Evos take their place in that line-up too, but not today.

Pans are simple enough motors, but have their idiosyncrasies. Shovels are easy enough to build as well, and also have their own unique characteristics. Both use a dome shaped piston, and match-

Jammer created this new/old Panhead by combining STD cases and heads with RevTech crank, S&S pistons and Andrews cam. 88 cubic inches of Retro.

ing combustion chamber that contribute much to their signature sounds. They are very different from the Evo, whose bathtub (or kidney) shaped chambers and flat top pistons changed their tune significantly. Each style of motor has their own tools and assembly processes, with Evos being possibly the easiest to assemble for the average mechanic.

The reliability and performance of the new motors is a definite plus, and parts are much easier to come by. S&S makes Panhead and Shovelhead cases to help you rebuild an old bike or they have new Shovelheads complete with the generator cases. The great thing about the new motors is you get old looks with today's technology, making the motor stronger and more reliable than any of the originals.

If you want a Shovel that will keep up with the latest Evos and TCs, try this 103 inch alternator engine with 5 inch stroke and 3-5/8 inch bore. Jammer

A Look Inside: S&S Shovel

If you're thinking about an early-style engine for that Bobber project, consider a new/old Shovelhead from S&S. By Borrowing design elements from the Evo, the S&S engineers were able to create a classic engine with Evolution-style valve train and oiling systems, one that uses Evo camshafts to boot. As S&S puts it: "You can get great Shovelhead looks with Evolution-style reliability and lower noise operation."

The S&S billet Shovelhead rocker boxes are engineered to work with H-D engines as well as S&S, by maintaining a 1.5:1 rocker arm ratio. What's shown here are a few photos from S&S that show the difference between the generator and alternator style engine. Even the generator style uses an alternator left side case, with an alternator to power the charging circuit. Either style will bolt up to a late model Softail-style inner primary and primary drive.

A Look Inside: S&S Shovel

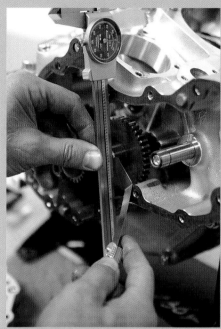

Whether the engine uses the typical alternator-style gear train or the earlier generator style, you still have to check the end play during final assembly.

Lifter blocks install just like they do on an Evolution. In fact, the engine uses Evo lifters.

Note the domed piston with cutouts for the 2.00 inch intake and 1.605 inch exhaust valves. The mark shown lets you know which is the cam side.

The Shovel, whether old or new, does not use long (Evo-style) bolts that pass through the cylinders to clamp the heads in place.

Instead, the Shovel uses one set of fasteners to hold the cylinder to the cases and another to bolt the head to the cast iron cylinder.

From S&S, the new Shovel comes with a Super E carb which is supported by this bracket on the back side.

By combining a new Evo style 100 inch RevTech engine with Xotic covers, Jammer has created a new twist on an old engine. Both Panhead and...

RETRO LOOKS WITH MODERN DEPENDABILITY

The look of a generator-style Shovelhead engine is undeniably cool. It's a classic design that will endure, but there is no reason that you can't have that look, and have modern features as well. That's what the S&S alternator/generator engines are all about. The most obvious advantage of an S&S alternator/generator engine is the alternator. There is no doubt that when the alternator electrical system was introduced in 1970, it was a giant step forward in capacity and dependability. Anyone who likes to use high-watt halogen headlights, or radios, or any of a long list of electrical accessories probably would not willingly go back to a generator charging system. It is also a fact that many electronic ignition systems don't function correctly if the battery is low. Any way you look at it, the dependability and additional output of an alternator is a real plus. If a generator is not used

on the engine, the generator location is an excellent place to mount a spin-on oil filter. There are other advantages to be had as well. High performance clutches, five and six speed transmissions, and many more drive train products are readily available for an alternator style engine, even one with a generator on the other side.

S&S alternator/generator engines are built from the same high quality components as their 93 inch Shovelhead engines, and have the same specifications. There is no difference in performance or dependability. Both high and low compression versions are available, and of course they all come complete with the new S&S billet rocker boxes and tappet guides. These engines contain Evolution® style camshafts which are designed for a generator style crankcase. These engines include the S&S Super Stock® Ignition and are covered by a two year parts and labor warranty.

Evolution motors are one of the most popular

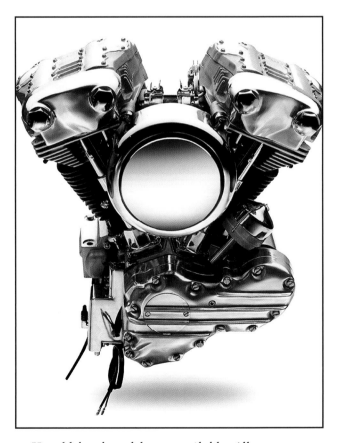

...Knucklehead models are available. All come completely assembled with "generator" style cam covers. Jammer

and versatile motors used today, with many different cubic inch configurations. You can get anything from a stock 80 inch up to a 145 inch motor. This allows for great variation if you are looking at a stock set up or if you are interested in adding some big horsepower. One big plus on Evolution engines is that any pre '99 soft-tail, and most all hardtail, frames are created with motor mounts that work with this motor. Problems can occur when using an Evo in a frame that was designed for a Pan or Knucklehead, the frame will need some modifications to fit the slightly bigger motor.

USED ENGINES:

The boom in custom bikes and bigger motors has been a blessing for a builder who does not need the huge horsepower motor with polished cases. Used Evolution motors are becoming more common and many are low mile power plants that were only taken out because of the owner's need

Accurate Engineering (located in Dolhan, Alabama) makes a variety of early-style engines, including these generator style Pans in displacements of 88, 93 and 103 inches.

Knuckleheads from Accurate can be ordered with the gloss black finish as shown, in displacements up to 106 cubic inches.

for speed. When buying a used engine, always ask to hear it run before you pay your money and take it home. I have heard of more than one guy getting the motor home, putting it in his frame, and then having major problems when the motor was fired up. The seller can then say it was your fault for doing something wrong, and you're left with the added expense of having the motor fixed.

If you are buying a motor that the seller claims to be rebuilt, ask to see all receipts and talk to the actual engine builder to get the scoop on the condition of the motor internally. If you do not do this, I would recommend taking the engine apart or having a trained mechanic do it to evaluate whether the motor is ready to go, or if there are issues inside that need to be addressed and repaired.

When titling time comes you also want to be sure your motor does not have case numbers that

Lee's Speed Shop

Engine builder Lee Wickstrom, (owner of the world's fastest gas-powered Knucklehead) runs Lee's Speed Shop located southwest of Minneapolis.

Lee Wickstrom is a fixture in the Minneapolis, St. Paul area. His shop, Lee's Speed Shop, is the official "go to" shop for cylinder head and porting work. Though best know for his porting work, Lee also does head repair work as well as overhauls on everything from Evos to Knuckles.

Given his experience, Lee seemed the ideal person to point out the possible pitfalls waiting for anyone trying to restore and repair an old V-Twin as part of a Bobber project.

Lee, how about a little background. How long have you been in the Business?

I've been rebuilding Harleys for 25 years and running Lee's for 10. Porting is the bulk of my work, but I do other cylinder head and engine work too.

Rebuilding any engine is a lot of work, are there special issues that come up when working on older engines, issues like metal fatigue, and stripped threads, and damage done by earlier rebuilds. And is one family of engines more prone to trouble than another?

In terms of the heads, it seems like Pan-heads are in the worst shape. I find cracks going from the spark-plug hole to a valve seat, or sometimes from the seat to a head-bolt hole. It's very common to find broken fins and stripped Pan-cover screws. Often I find the bronze valve seats sunk deeply into the head. Then I may

machine the head and install a new seat. But if there are cracks in the seat area I wonder - will the new seat stay installed? Is it worth spending a thousand dollars to repair two heads or should I recommend that the customer buy two new heads for about the same money.

Are parts readily available for the older engines?

I can't think of anything I can't get. Maybe some Flathead stuff, but even then you can get most parts.

Is it a lot more money to rebuild a Pan or Shovel, than an Evo?

Yes, generally it's way more for labor, and usually more for parts too. The engines are older, they've run more miles, and parts cost more.

How does a person decide whether it's better to buy and repair an old engine, like a Pan or Shovel, or just buy a new one?

It depends on the motor, and the owner. If you have a tired Pan or Shovel, you probably can't rebuild it for the price of a new Evo. But if you buy the Evo, then you don't have a Pan or Shovel.

How does a person avoid buying a motor that needs way too much work?

It's best if you can hear it run, otherwise you don't know if it's going to smoke like crazy or if it has a knock. That's a good rule of thumb, unless you're buying it really cheap and can afford to spend thousands of dollars fixing the engine.

What's the best value in a used Harley-Motor?

Ironhead Sportys are still pretty cheap, but you have to be careful. You can easily spend more to repair the engine than you did for the bike. A friend bought a complete older Sportster for fifteen hundred dollars and all it needs is the top end freshened, that's a pretty good deal. At the same time, you will probably never get all your money out of an Ironhead.

What are some mistakes you see people make when they try to rebuild or restore an old engine?

The number one issue I see in old engines is

Lee's Speed Shop

engine cases where the serial number has been tampered with, especially on Pans and Knuckles. Customers bring in a motor to me for work on and I won't - 'cause the numbers aren't right. In Minnesota it's a felony to have them in your possession. So don't buy an engine if the numbers don't look right, or find someone who's familiar with the H-D numbers to look for you.

Let's walk through some options for people who want to (or have to) buy new components?

For Pans and Shovels, heads are around a thousand for a set. With Knuckleheads, things go way up. V-twin and Flathead Power both make new Knuckleheads. It's over three thousand dollars for two heads. To build a Knuckle from new parts is around ten thousand dollars.

I know you build some new Knuckles, Shovels and Pans for people. Can you talk a little about your preference for parts and some of the options?

If you're building a new Knucklehead, you can start with S&S cases and bottom end, the parts are very good quality. S&S also makes a nice cam cover. From there it depends on the displacement. Flathead Power makes a bunch of different bore sizes. You can have 3-5/8 inch, up to 4-inch, cylinders. In fact, they sell a 120 cubic inch Knuckle. All that stuff is spendy though. For a reasonable price, you should stick with stock bore, maybe a stroker. If you add to the performance, it adds to the price.

What about Pans and Shovels?

For Pans, the STD heads cost more, but they're good quality. They come set up for a Shovel-style intake, for more performance. For the bottom end I use all S&S. For Shovelheads, STD and S&S both make heads, but the S&S heads are less money. S&S makes that new Shovel engine, which is a good value.

What are the mistakes people make when they try to use old engines for their Bobber project?

Sometimes they come in here all excited about a Knucklehead-Bobber. When they find out what the motor's going to cost they loose their enthusiasm. And the old motors need more maintenance. They have solid lifters, points ignition, kick start and generator. You need to be fairly mechanical to own one. The kickstart is something to take into account when you're building this motor, if it's a really big engine with high compression it's going to be a lot harder to kick over than a low compression 74-inch motor..

Old and new Shovelheads. With old engines it can be more to repair a head than to replace it with new.

Where else are you going to see a Flathead cylinder and head set up on the flow bench?

One of Lee's Shovels, built with alternator left side case and modern flywheel ass'm, meaning this Shovel bolts up to a modern inner primary and 6-speed.

55

Huey Schwebs (Cleveland Motorcycle Company, hdhuey@aol.com) says, "real Bobbers need Flathead engines." The example seen here, mounted in a Redneck Bobber frame, dates from 1944 and displaces 80 cubic inches. Jim at Karata came up with the unique belt primary...

...that allows Huey to combine the Flathead with a 5-speed tranny (and electric start). Milled tranny cover and distributor are the work of Jesse at Cleveland, while the external belt cover is from Crime Scene Choppers.

have been altered, which is a big red flag for the DMV, i.e. this could be a stolen motor. Always buy from trusted, respected companies if at all possible to avoid any "shady" deals. It would be a major bummer to lose your bike after you spent many hours of time, and a lot of hard earned cash, building it.

If buying a used vintage motor, many considerations must be taken. Although old Harley-Davidson motors are drawing big money on the market these days, don't let the price tags fool you. Many of the parts are in need of major welding or repair - despite the big prices. Gone is the day when you could find a cheap basket case to build. Today we have overblown pricing and E-bay bidders who have driven prices through the roof. If you want to go vintage, be prepared to pay high prices for the parts and be equally prepared to spend more money to have the parts repaired to a usable state (note the comments of Lee from Lee's Speed Shop).

Always examine closely the cases and castings for any cracks, dings, nicks or repairs. The old-style castings are not always clean and flawless which opens the door to problems. If you take your time, and do your research, and ask around you should be able to determine if the pieces you are looking at are worth the money or not. As stated earlier, be cautious with swap meet parts, you may be opening a can of worms that you are not prepared to deal with. It's generally better to go through a reputable motorcycle shop or parts dealer. Many fly-by-night, swap-meet deals may not be deals at all, but will cost you money when the motor gets confiscated. If you do attend swap meets, look for the vendors that also own legitimate bike shops. These guys know their reputation is at stake and will not normally jeopardize their business by selling stolen parts. These same shops are also valuable resources, you can ask questions about items you may see at other booths, the honest guys will usually be happy to help you out.

LEGAL ISSUES

Any new motor or cases you buy should come with an MSO (Manufacturer's Statement of Origin) showing who manufactured the motor. Much like a title card, the MSO lists the buyer and seller, be sure any previous transfers are noted on the MSO. Similar to the frame process, be sure you have all your bases covered here before walking into the DMV.

If the motor is used and does not have a title, the buyer needs to check that the motor is not

The RevTech crate motors come plain, black-wrinkle or polished. The 88 inch engine is a very good value for budget conscious Bobber builders.

registered as stolen or has any leans against it. They would then need to get a Bill of Sale from the seller proving that they did indeed buy the motor from said party. All information should be recorded as to who it was purchased from, their address and phone number. This is in case any legal problems would arise after you try and title the bike with the used motor.

Also be aware that if you already have a fully titled bike with the correct numbers, swapping the motor out for a different motor, one that does not have the proper paperwork, will only result in losing your bike. At big rallies, such as Sturgis, there are police officers who spend all their time looking through the sea of bikes to find mis-matched motors and frames. By running the plate on your bike they can quickly match what the title states to what you actually have in the bike. If the numbers don't match or there is reason to suspect modified numbers, be prepared to say goodbye bike.

A new factory Evo from a company like Dumbassbiker.com (that's a real name) is another great value. 80 cubic inches of torque and reliability.

Chapter Six

Transmissions

Four, Five or Six Speeds?

The transmission, which transfers the power from the motor to the rear wheel, is something that should be thought about in detail before making a decision as to which model to buy. Although a great old-skool transmission would be the traditional four-speed, kick-start running jockey shift, this system offers many more safety risks than a typical foot shift setup. And for long road trips, or high speed traveling, the jockey shift can cause major headaches. The

Whether it's an old 4-speed or a late-model six-speed, new gears, shafts and components are as close as your local parts shop. Biker's Choice

four-speed H-D transmission, used from 1936 to 1984, evolved from gate shift, to ratchet top, then rotary top. The four-speed is the preference for the true old skool crowd, and often has a kicker already installed. However, if you don't already have one in hand they often cost more than the newer five-speeds.

The suicide setup should be reserved for the experienced rider who can handle the added risks. A more modern, efficient option is the five and six-speed transmissions which are manufactured by a wide variety of companies. These provide a nice low first gear to get off the line quick, but also keep the rpm's down in high gear. The five-speed transmission came into production through Harley in 1980. Although the four-speed was still used on some models, the five-speed eventually took over for good when the four-speed was dropped from production.

There are five and six-speed transmissions available in the traditional four-speed case if you want the vintage look, otherwise new Softail-style transmissions can be used in almost any rigid frame designed to accept pre-'99 drivetrain. By using an adjustable transmission plate you can mate new-style transmissions to old-style frames, to add new technology to old skool class. An adjustable

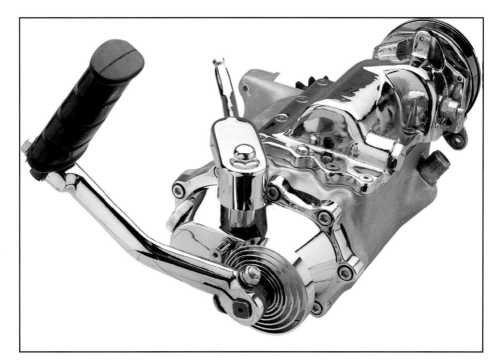

These 4-speed transmissions are built from RevTech cases and close-ratio gear sets. Fit most 4-speed frames when mated to '70 to '84 running gear. Available with 2 different first gear ratios, for FX or FL applications. Jammer

These '36 to'64, 4-speed, kicker transmissions are ideal for bikes running a tin primary. Available with 2 different first gear ratios. Designed for chain final drive. Jammer

plate is recommended to allow for perfect alignment of the transmission with the primary.

VARIOUS TRANSMISSION STYLES & SPECS

A few comments on transmissions: H-D, Big Twin four-speed transmissions are basically the same except the FX models, which came with different ratios than the FLH models. Also, the clutch pushrods varied as follows: '41-'64 used a 13 inch rod. '65-'69 used a 13-1/4 inch rod. '70-'75 used a rod measuring 13-7/8 inches. '75-'84 used a rod with a dimension of 13-3/4 inch.

The pushrod length started to change when electric start was added (the mainshaft became longer). There were some different throwout bearings used along the way as well, which necessitated a longer or shorter clutch pushrod. I still prefer the early style, before they went to the less heavy-duty, wafer-style throwout bearing. The older style lasts forever, while the later-style has a snap-ring that often comes off and the bearing is a poor design. The ratchet-style shift top worked well but then came the cow-pie style and even though the linkage set up is sloppy, it shifted

smoothly. Five-speeds mainly added a closer ratio and are better yet. Most people think they're getting more top end gearing out of a five-speed, but both use a one-to-one top gear. A five-speed offers closer shifting ratios and is generally smoother and easier on the gear train. Six-speeds provide a nice low first gear and an overdrive sixth, though the actual overdrive ratio changes from one brand and model to another. The right-side-drive five and six-speeds came about when tires went to 230 and 250, no longer did builders have to offset the transmission to the right by as much as an inch. In my opinion, a 200 rear is as big as it should get on a Bobber.

There are the "retro" four-speed transmissions which come in different configuration for four, five, and six-speed gearing. There is the ratchet top, rotary top, and the jockey lid style. But if you're reading this book the last thing you will be worrying about is the over-the-top fat tires, skinny is the way to go!

Weyland form Solutions Machining gave me some information on the differences in the various transmissions: "There's a large amount of hype with regard to four, five, and six-speed transmissions. Many of these claim to be better for nothing other than that extra gear or two that you pay for. Here's the bottom line as far as I'm concerned - I don't care if you have TEN gears. The two most important issues are where (in the rpm range) it calls for shifting with regard to your riding style, and the final gear ratio."

For many, many years people automatically assumed that because a transmission had five or six-gears that they were over-drive transmissions. Wrong.

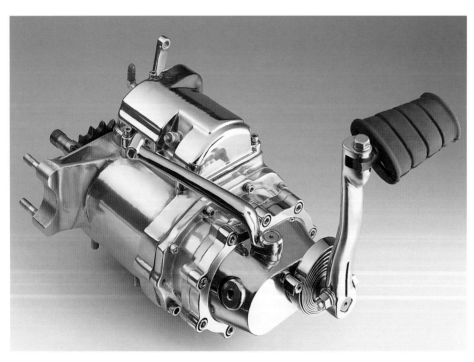

Have your cake and eat it too. A 4-speed case that holds a 5-speed gearset. Works with most '70 to '84 bikes with electric-start and forward controls. Custom Chrome

Nowadays, there are overdrive gear sets available, but you need to be aware when shopping for a transmission so you get exactly what you want. In the end, like most other things, it's all a matter of personal preference.

Four-speeds (when built properly) last just fine. They do, however, require more attention to detail as far as maintaining proper tolerances is concerned. Still, their design and aesthetic reflects an era when craftsmanship was valued over production numbers. This aesthetic is immediately evident when one sets an early transmission next to a late one. Five-speeds are more of a "Lego-block" type of transmission, and are obviously more cost effective to produce. That said, they have evolved to be a pretty serviceable transmission, even if they do lack any inherent aesthetic appeal.

MATCH TRANSMISSION TO THE FRAME

It is important to be sure, whatever transmission you choose, that it will bolt up correctly in your frame. Custom rigid frames are available which can use softtail-style Harley-Davidson transmissions, or the older four-speed style transmission, with the need of only the proper transmission plate. Five and six-speed transmissions use the same mounting configuration so they will fit any rigid, seatpost style frames, or softail

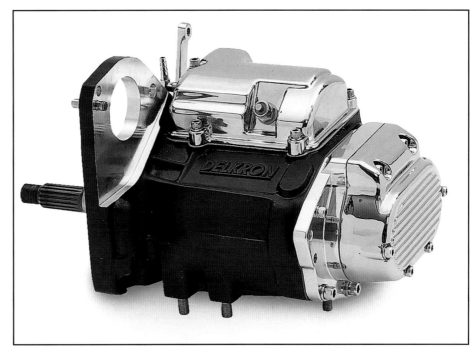

Sturdy Delkron case holds heavy-duty, 5-speed, American made gears. Fits all Softail-style frames. Biker's Choice

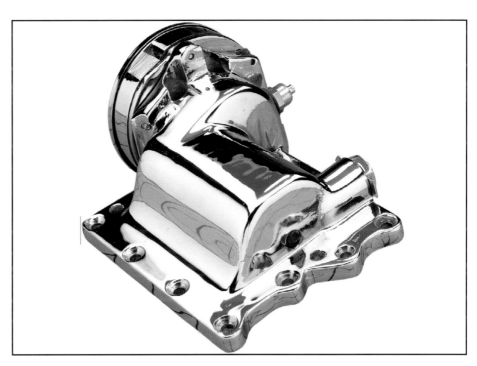

If your old '52 through '79, 4-speed tranny is in need of a new ratchet top, look no further than the Jammer catalog. Comes with forward-control-style drum. Order yours in chrome or polished finish.

frames built before 1999 when the Twin Cam was introduced. Most of the rigid frames out there utilize the same components as the Evolution Softail, but be aware '99 and up Twin Cam parts will not work without major modifications.

A frame such as the ones Sucker Punch Sally's, or Spartan Frameworks, sell will accept four, five, or six-speed transmissions, as long as you use the correct transmission plate. Companies are now realizing what a wide variety of custom parts are being used to build bikes so adjustable transmission plates can be purchased which allow for any of the three styles of transmission to be used. Hank Young offers a great, high quality, adjustable plate that we used to fit our transmissions in our four-speed rigid frames (our school project bikes farther along in the book).

I asked George Counes, of Spartan Frameworks, about the frames he builds and the transmission options and this is what he said: "I build all my frames with four-speed transmission

mounts. The four-speed mounting system is stronger than the five or six-speed setup. I like four-speeds (except cow-pies), as they are better for a jockey setup, the kicker doesn't look like an afterthought, the final drive is the same as a five-speed, you don't have to cut the starter bracket off, and best of all, you can put a slop-top lid on for every day riding and then throw a ratchet lid on for drag racing. To mount the five and six-speed transmissions in my frames requires a 3/8 inch thick transmission adapter plate, that way you can mate my a four-speed frame with a five-speed transmission."

"For the five and six-speed transmissions I put a relief in the seat post to clear the lid, and the fifth-mount is slightly foreword. This would have to be done to most four-speed frames to accommodate a five or six-speed. The five and six-speed, and right-side-drive transmissions mount to the frame in the same way. A five or six-speed kick-only transmission can be mounted in my frames without the use of a motor plate or an aluminum primary and the transmission plate or the frame will not break."

"As for stock or other after market five-speed frames running a five or six-speed transmission with no inner primary or motor plate, I gusset and beef-up the whole area under the transmission mounts to make sure the mounts won't fail."

SUICIDE - NOT FOR BEGINNERS

They call them "suicide" set ups for a reason, it is more dangerous! A true suicide shift refers to a non-rocker-clutch style set up where the bike must be put in neutral if you want to come to a stop and take your foot off the clutch. This set

The original Jockey lid on my 4-speed suicide set-up is definitely not for beginners. Inexperienced riders would have a hard time finding gears as you can slide from 1st to 4th since there is no ratchet style shifter drum.

up is not for the faint of heart, and should only be used by riders who know their bikes well and know how to ride. Combine suicide shift and no front brake, and your daily rides become a quest to just make it to your destination safely. When stopped on a hill with a suicide set up, you must really be in tune with your bike and the clutch system to keep from stalling.

More and more Bobbers are showing up with a hydraulic clutch as part of the suicide set up, as seen on this Ted Tine bike. Makes for a very neat installation.

Also, if you have no front brake, it is even more difficult to hold the bike still while you try and step on the clutch, get the bike in gear, and get it moving forward without rolling back into the car behind you, or stalling the motor. This set up is NOT recommended for a novice rider and should only be attempted by experienced, skilled riders who can handle running this set up without having to think too much.

I have had this set up on my Panhead since the first day I built it, and I will admit to avoiding certain streets and hills for a while until I felt comfortable riding the bike and operating the clutch system. Now when I ride it I don't even think about it and can stop and start anywhere without problems. When I am riding along with friends they are amazed how quickly and smoothly I can shift the bike with the suicide set up, almost as if I was running a foot shift. Like anything, practice makes perfect and the more you ride and practice the better you will get. The rocker clutch style allows the rider to lock

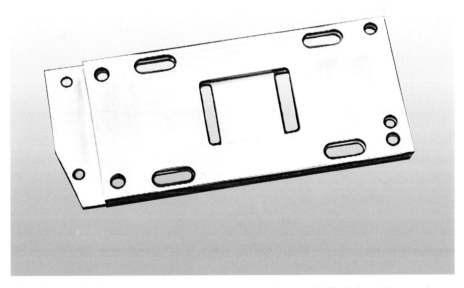

This 4-speed, chrome transmission mounting plate is drilled for either early or late transmission tabs. Jammer

Baker Klassic Kicker Gears are cut in the US of A, then heat treated to prevent failure. Fit '36 to '86, 4-speed transmissions. Baker

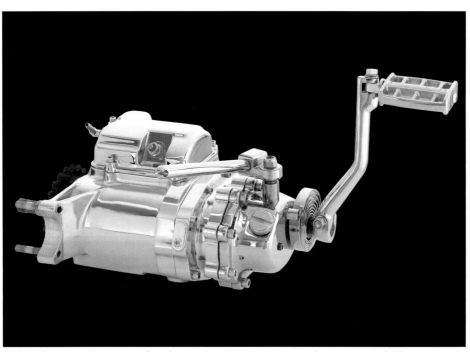

This direct replacement for the stock '70 to '84 4-speed uses a 1:1 fifth gear and an overdrive sixth (.86:1), which drops the rpm by 500 rpm at a given speed on the highway. Bolts up to the frame and inner primary like a stock tranny, may interfere with stock exhaust and starter bracket on the right side. Baker

the clutch in, which lets them put both feet down at a stop while the bike is still in gear. This was a standard piece of equipment on the older Harleys that utilized a hand shift. Although it does allow a bit more room for error on the rider's part it should not be taken to be the magic fix all for hand-shifting issues.

TRANSMISSION OPTIONS - BAKER DRIVETRAIN

Baker Drivetrain's contributions to the Old Skool are the best-kept secret in the business. Known for premium drivetrain innovations found on newer custom bikes, or later stock H-Ds, Baker Drivetrain also produces a high quality six-into-four gearset to improve upon old technologies.

The Baker six-into-four is a 1970-to-early-1984 Shovelhead four-speed case that houses a Baker Overdrive six-Speed gearset. The six-into-four is available with or without the kicker assembly which includes both a stock rubber kick pedal and a brass pedal. It features the new Baker Klassic Kicker Gears, which are a smoother, stronger, and quieter improvement to the current OEM replacement gears made offshore. These gears are also available separately. This transmission is available with a raw, show polished, or wrinkle black case and a 33-tooth pulley. Baker Klassic Kicker Gears are an American made alternative to the offshore monopoly on OEM 1936-1984 kicker gears. Features include: Rounded teeth for smoother, quieter rolling and a reinforced stop-peg to prevent breakage in the transmission. All the gears are made from 4140 heat-treated steel

A N-1 Racing Shift Drum on a Bobber? Yes, this is great for bikes with foot clutches. A N-1 shift pattern, which is a pattern with neutral before first gear instead, of neutral between first and second, eliminates the hope and guessing of finding neutral before you have to take your foot off the clutch and step on the ground for balance when stopping. That is, "neutral is all the way down to get your foot planted on the ground." This is especially helpful with jockey shift linkage that loses a lot of the "feel" when looking for conventional neutral. Baker has found this to be a handy and popular solution to embarrassing stalls or slamming into stopped cars.

The Baker Special Request six-Speed "Franken-tranny" for Softails, is a special transmission with a six-into-four door, which allows a kicker assembly and a sixth gear on a Softail five-speed case. It's your choice whether or not to have the starter ear removed for kick-only applications. Call Baker for more details.

Other Old Skool components include an outer bearing support for six-into-four transmissions and a hydraulic clutch actuator for six-into-four or conventional four-speed transmissions.

For that retro, suicide shift Bobber you need a suicide style clutch pedal. Jammer

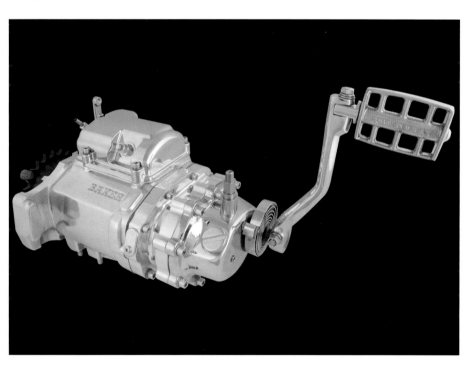

The Frankentranny is another kick-equipped model designed for Softail applications. Mount for starter can be removed for kick-only applications (as shown). Baker

Chapter Seven

Primary Drive

Chains & Belts

The choice of primary drive, chain or belt, depends on your personal taste and the type of motor and transmission you are running in your bike. Although the enclosed tin primary of the old bikes is a tried and true system, the mean look of the open belt drive has been extremely popular for many years. Some of the old skool builders have even removed the tin primaries to expose the chain drives for a more mechanical look. Be aware of the safety concerns associated with open belts,

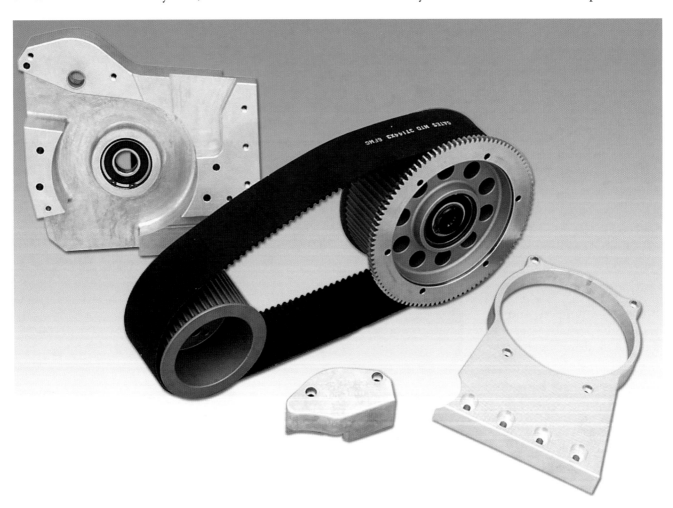

The Brute IV from Primo is one heavy duty belt drive, with a 3 inch belt, Alto clutch assembly, and two-piece "inner primary" (to make alignment easier). Designed to accommodate electric start.

however. If not covered properly they can, and will, catch pant legs and have the ability to inflict serious harm. Almost everyone who runs on open belt will have at least a couple pair of jeans with ripped and tattered pant legs. In my opinion, if you are fairly new to riding motorcycles, run an enclosed primary until you have enough experience to be able to safely use an open belt. At least use a cover on the belt.

The early tin primary setup was used until 1964. The cast aluminum housing was introduced, along with electric start, in 1965. This newer setup, with the four-speed transmission, was used until 1984, and variations are still used with the five-speed transmission right up to the present.

Besides the aesthetic appeal, a belt-drive primary system makes it easier to match up an old engine with a newer transmission. You don't have to find exactly the right inner primary and all the related parts to connect the two components.

I talked with Lee, of Broadway Choppers, and got his opinion on primaries and how to tell one from another. "First, my favorite is chain, chain, chain. Hell, I think they wrote a song. Anyway, on early bikes which are Panheads (the mighty great ones) I like to see you on a '58 and up if possible, with the updated bearings in the engine, but let's talk about primaries. The three basic pri-

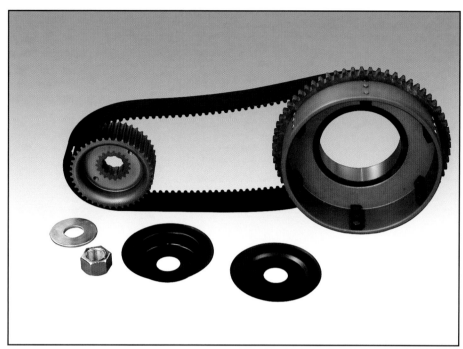

From BDL comes this 1-1/2 inch belt drive meant to fit most Shovelheads. Will accept a stock clutch or BDL's own heavy duty unit. Kustomwerks

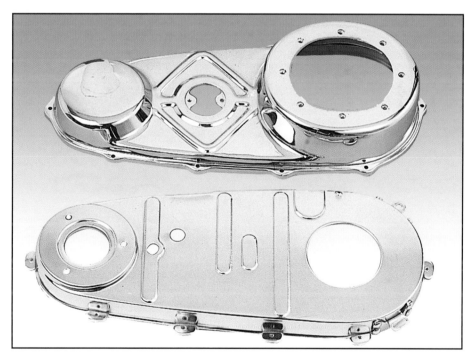

This new, chrome tin primary set comes in various configurations to fit most 4-speed bikes (non electric start) from '55 to '84. Kustomwerks

Meant for kick-only applications (note the missing ring gear), this 3 inch wide BDL belt and clutch assembly is available for Pans, Shovels, and early and late Evos. Kustomwerks

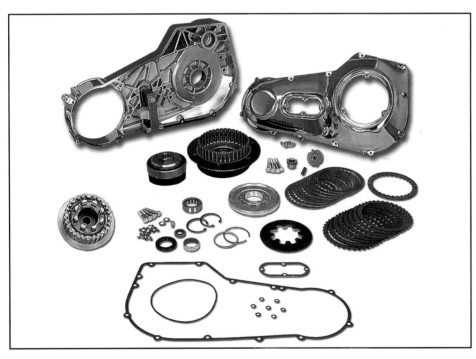

Sometimes it's easier to buy all the parts for one assembly as a kit. This chain primary assembly will fit Evo Softail drivetrains, either '90 to '93 or '94 to '97. Kustomwerks

maries are: '36-'54, '55-'64 and '65-'69. On the generator engines the '36-'54 is most notable. If you are swap meet shopping, the '36 to '54 has the small hole at the engine end. A '55-'69 primary uses a bigger hole for the bigger-bearing engine. The '65 and up elect-start engine is deeper yet at the engine side."

"It seems most new guys to the Chopper scene, and at least half the old ones like belts, they look cool. If you run a belt, remember alignment, alignment, alignment. Belts are non-forgiving. I've seen used fluorescent light bulbs used as a straight edge, when you're doing the assembly in the garage on a non-stop mission, and can't wait to get a real straight edge. Don't think the alignment will be OK if you just eye-ball it for now, and that you can come back later and fix it. Eye-ball is not good enough and most guys don't go back in and fix it 'till it breaks. It's not important how I know this."

"Four-speeds forever. In the real world of building at home, four-speed style bikes break down into four styles:

1) '64 and down, pre electric start. These have a 11-3/4 inch shaft coming out of the tranny and run a 13-1/4 inch pushrod.

2) Then you have the early electric start with the 12 inch tranny shaft and a 13-5/8 inch push rod.

3) Next you have the '70-'74 style, which uses a 12-1/2 inch shaft and a 14 inch push rod.

4) Then you will have the late '75 and up models, which also use a 12-1/2 inch shaft out of the tranny and an even longer, 14-1/8 inch pushrod. This is what some call the beginning of the end, where the new throwout bearing came in."

"Now the reason you see the longer length main-shaft is due to changes in the design of the bike. The '64 and down bikes were kick-start only. In '65 the electric start came in so they needed more room on the mainshaft. In '70 the cone engine was introduced."

"If you're building a bike from swap meet parts, ebay or the parts pile you scored, here's the deal: '54 on down, the engine sprocket shaft is shorty keyway style. '55-'64, uses a 3-1/2 inch long spline and thread. '65-'69, uses a 3-3/4 inch long spline and threaded section. '70-'71 is 4-1/4 inches long splined and threaded section. In '72 they went to a larger diameter and dropped the Keyway and stayed that way 'till mid '81, which was commonized and used a different taper."

"Don't fall into the 4 in a 5 myth unless you fall into a good deal on one compared to what you're gonna spend on that dirty OEM tranny that bubba discarded when he

Another complete primary kit, this one meant to match up a modern Pan or Shovel with a 4-speed tranny, includes 1-1/2 inch BDL belt assembly. Jammer

This open belt primary kit includes an electric starter and the necessary support brackets. Works with original 4-speed cases, as well as modern 6-in-a-4 cases. Jammer

Another primary belt, this time from Primo, with anodized pulleys and a fiberglass reinforced belt. Fits Shovels and Pans. Jammer

bought the 4 in a 5. Gear it and love it, you can do this through the engine sprocket or tranny. Gear according to your needs, one or two teeth is a big jump. If going taller on the tranny watch your clearance on the ratchet lid, a 26 tooth sprocket will fit but look close as Murphy is always close by. If you go for the cool factor and run a belt primary you will most likely have to change your sprocket, as it changes the primary ratio most times. Look for 1.60 to 1 reduction or if taller gearing is required, go to 1.55 to 1."

"There may be many reasons certain people do or don't run a belt system. One of the problems with the open belt primary, I believe, is that it puts undue stress, and wear and tear, on the motor and transmission compared to a chain style. The open belt is run with much more tension than a chain and with 3 inch belts on the older style set ups, where no inner primary plate is used, the bearings are definitely under more stress."

"Although I do run open belts on my bikes and have not seen any immediate problems, the configuration of the open belt on the old four-speed set up with no backing plate has to be a bit harder on the components. There are positives of running a belt drive besides just the aesthetic value. Belt drives do run relatively smoothly compared to the chain counterpart, and you never have to worry about oil leaks from the pri-

Though we all like the look of an open belt, the outside cover helps keep your jeans out of the belt and the belt off your ankle or calf.

mary. With smaller width belts you also can run them open or closed but beware that they do get extremely hot, so if you do run them enclosed, vent holes must be used or the belt will not last long. Belt drive systems also make it easier to mix and match older style engines with newer style transmissions. This is a great idea if you plan on taking your old Pan or Shovel on some long distance trips where freeway speeds may be run for long periods of time."

"Some of the disadvantages of the belt include the greater risk of failure, a broken belt is a quick way to bring a road trip to a stop. If the belt is run open, rocks and other road debris have the chance to get into the belt and cause premature wear or damage to the belt. Belts are expensive so replacing them often can be very hard on the checkbook. Before you get your parts ordered, it is important to check the various manufacturers and gather as much information as possible to get the right system for your bike. For example, the older style Panheads have tapered shafts, as opposed to the newer style Pans which have the spline shaft, know what you have so you order the right parts!"

"Companies like Primo, BDL, and Karata have web sites to look through, or the parts are offered for sale in most of the big catalogs. These companies are working hard to keep up with the current needs, and the old faithful designs, so no matter what you plan to run, they make a system that fits."

"The chain system utilizes an enclosed casing that houses the chain, a tension adjuster and the oil needed to keep everything lubricated properly. Chains do stretch, so routine checks of chain slop is a must to keep everything running smoothly. One great thing about chains drives, if proper preventative maintenance is routinely done, they can last almost the entire life of the bike. One disadvantage of the chain is the fact that most end up leaking some primary oil and once it starts it's often hard to get the primary case sealed up again."

"Connecting the motor to the transmission can be a simple task, if planned properly, or a nightmare if incorrect parts are used. Certain configurations will run stock style primary systems while others may require custom ones to match the different year or style components. If you buy the incorrect inner or outer primary it will become apparent rather quickly as you try to line up and bolt everything together. The best place to start would be your local motorcycle shop where you can browse through catalogs from Drag Specialties and Custom Chrome, to look at different systems available for sale. Often a full kit can be purchased taking the guess work out of what you need to match your motor and transmission combo if you're using an Evolution motor. Pans and Shovels do not have as many options as the Evolution, so you will need to do a little searching to find the correct inner primary that will work with one of the earlier engines."

If you don't want an open primary, but like the idea of a belt, try this 8mm Primo system meant to work as an enclosed assembly on Big Twins (Shovelheads) from '78 to '84.

Bobber Gallery

In The Eye of the Beholder

Built by Ted Tine of Ted Tine Motorsports fame, the Bobber seen here is perhaps a perfect blend of old skool and new. Though powered by an Evo, the bike definitely has that old skool look. And while the clutch is foot-operated, the linkage is hydraulic. "I wanted something that looked like what I used to ride back in high school in the early 70s," says Ted. "I just started with all the cast-off stuff that was lying around the shop and this is what happened."

The cast off stuff included some pretty nice pieces, like a complete prototype TTM frame, a pair of original Panhead tanks, and a damaged dash from a '38 Knucklehead.

The tanks and dash are the foundation for this Bobber. "Paul Gamache helped us with fabrica-

A unique mix of old and new. Ted's Bobber uses fat, 16 inch tires on both ends and old sheet metal, to establish the old skool profile. The mostly modern running gear (96 inch Evo and 6-speed transmission with belt drive to the rear wheel) keeps it running reliably down the road. Photos by Dino Petrocelli

tion," explains Ted, "he repaired, split and stretched the original dash so it would run the full length of the tanks. We also enlarged the hole so the dash could house an Autometer electronic speedo driven by the sensor in the six-speed tranny."

While the bike might look like what Ted rode thirty years ago, it's way more sophisticated than anything Ted (or anyone else) built at the time. The forward controls, complete with custom "ventilation," are from Accutronix. The left side master cylinder connects through a nearly invisible hydraulic line to a Ness hydraulic clutch cover. Likewise invisible is all the wiring and the internal throttle.

Ted's Bobber rolls on two, sixteen-inch original H-D wheels, powder coated black and re-laced. The front tire reads 16X3 while the rear is a relatively wide 200 series, both from Avon. The nifty seat with the yellow stitching is the work of Christine LePera.

Whether it's old skool or new, doesn't matter. Ted's Bobber definitely wins the people's choice award. "This bike always draws a crowd," says Ted, "and lots of people want to buy this bike,"

The hand shifter has its own interesting story, "We were digging through an old box of parts and found this really neat shift lever. It looked like it was designed for the bike. So I had the holes drilled and mounted it on the bike and then found out later that it's an original shifter from a '57 'Vette. The shifter is probably worth more than the whole bike."

The super bright yellow paint is taxicab yellow from PPG, applied by Bob Gorske from Roade Studio.

"I like my bikes to have brakes on both ends, with 2 master cylinders, none of that integrated-brake stuff."

73

Knucklehead Power

Lee from Lee's Speed Shop (Chapter Five) likes to take a break from building engines, and build complete bikes instead. Most could be called old-skool bikes with a certain flair. The Knucklehead seen here definitely goes over the top.

"My aim was to use new technology while keeping an old skool feel," says Lee. The frame is a 35-degree rigid from Chopper Guys. Rolling stock includes a laced 21-inch front tire on a spoked rim and a 230/60/16 rear mounted to a PMFR wheel. Sitting on the top tube is a factory XL tank stretched by Jerry Sherer (also responsible for the orange paint) while the rear fender is a flat trailer model.

Given Lee's occupation, it's not surprising that this bike is all about the motor. The Knuckle started as a set of S&S cases and five-inch, 'wheels. Bolted to the cases are cylinders from Flathead Power with a bore of 3-13/16 inches. The combination of bore and stoke nets out to 114 cubic inches. The heads are likewise from FHP. What really sets this Knuckle apart, however, are the two "97" carbs mounted on the left side. The intake manifold is a custom part created through the joint efforts of Lee and John Trutnau from PMFR. As Lee explains, "I machined the base and John fabricated the rest from thick aluminum plate so the corners could be rounded to give it a cast appearance." So the bike, and the manifold, look like they were built in '50s.

Nothing looks as good as a Knucklehead. What makes this machine special is the displacement, and the little tricks like the Crane HI-4 ignition hidden in the distributor housing.

Short and stocky like any good Bobber, Lee's creation uses an H-D front fork with factory front brake caliper and rotor. Belt drive is connected to a four-speed transmission and includes a provision for electric start.

The carburetors are the hot rodders favorite: Stromberg "97s," mounted to a hand-fabricated manifold that only appears to be cast.

Old Bike from New Parts

Old Shit has an undeniable allure to any true motorhead. We all want a genuine, steel '32 Ford body and a real Panhead engine. But they only made something like 60,000 Deuces, and the newest Panhead was built in 1965.

When County Line Choppers decided to build an old-skool Bobber, they decided to build it from new components. No rust, no metal fatigue and parts that were, well, new. They also decided to add a few unique touches of their own.

The Panhead engine is a 2005 model, and though the MSO bears a stamp from STD, the components came from a variety of companies like S&S, Andrews and JIMS.

The transmission is also new, and carries five forward gears, one kicker and an electric starter. Shifting is by hand, and the clutch is foot operated through a hydraulic linkage. A fat BDL belt connects the two major driveline components, with a motor plate on the inside and a cover on the outside.

The frame from Kraftec and CLC is short and squatty with only two extra inches in the top tube and a rake of 38 degrees. Bolted on top is a hand-fabricated tank. What's more significant is the very cool grille, also fabricated at the CLC shop. You wouldn't think a grille and a hood ornament would look good on a Bobber, but somehow they work.

In fact, the whole thing can only be called bitchin', which just goes to show that there's more than one way to build an old skool Bobber.

Can a Bobber be art-deco? This one is, with one-off grille, prominent hood ornament and fabricated air cleaner. Paint on Lady Luck is by JT's Customs, seat work by Duane Ballard.

The rear wheel measures 18X5.5 inches while the front measures 21X3.5 inches. Tires by Metzeler, rear caliper by Exile.

Headlight by Adjure, note the painted bars, Ness grips and the "hood ornament." Photos by Dino Petrocelli.

A Complete Make Over

Some people start their Bobber projects with a pile of parts, others start with an imperfect, old-style motorcycle. Gennaro Sepe describes his original bike as a "typical mid-'80s deal, a wishbone-Paughco frame and a motor that was half Delkron bottom end and half Shovelhead top end."

The two biggest changes Gennaro made are to the frame and the motor. With help from a friend by the name of Hot Rod Bill (Krwirko), Gennaro cut out and reinforced the frame's top tube, primarily so he could eliminate the reinforcing tube that ran underneath. He and Hot Rod also cut off all the brackets and tabs on the frame except one, and converted the upper motor-mount to an open-V.

"I wanted a real Harley-Davidson Panhead," explains Gennaro, "and when I bought this one I knew it needed a complete rebuild. I sent everything to Weyland at Solutions Machining and he repaired the cases and heads and installed all new S&S internals. With the stroker bottom end the motor now displaces 84 cubic inches.

A period correct bike needs a period correct paint job, done in this case with House of Kolor materials by Jerry and Andy Didio from Marty and Sons.

A "skinny belt" connects the engine and 4-speed transmission. Handle bars are narrowed drag-bars mounted to Flanders risers. Sparto taillight mounts to a recycled rear fender.

The transmission is a '70s vintage four-speed." The rear fender is about as old skool as you can get. The boys took two spare tire covers from a '36 Ford, welded them together, and molded in the area where the taillight mounts. The gas tank is what Gennaro calls a "Friscoed XL." An offset-style Springer fork supports a 21 inch rim laced to a Star hub. In back a sixteen inch FX rim is wrapped by a 130 tire. Not everyone could see the Bobber, disguised as a mid-'80s Chopper, but Gennaro could.

Eric Gorgeous from Vodoo Cycles gets credit for the special XL tank. Note the suicide clutch and hand shift, and the "window paned" neck area.

Though Rod Grimme is only in his mid-thirties, he's got an undeniable old-skool attitude. When it came time to build a motorcycle, nothing but the real thing would do. "I don't like what they call Choppers today." says Rod. "I collected my parts over time, you can still get good deals on old parts, if you're willing to wait for that one good deal. I found most of my parts at swap meets and over the Internet."

Nearly all the parts on Rod's bike are either original factory parts from the late '40s to the early '50s, or genuine aftermarket parts from the '70s. "I've got this one Chopper magazine from 1972, and there's a Panhead in there that served as the basis of my plan."

Rod's Panhead engine is the real deal, manufactured in 1949. "I bought it in pieces, and some of those pieces had to be sent out to specialists for repair before we could do the rebuild." Rod goes on to explain that the hardtail frame is a factory item, "that's someplace between a '49 and a '53, and the four-speed transmission is a '48." There was only one choice for a front fork, a twisted-leg Springer, supporting a 21-inch rim and Speedmaster tire. In back Rod used a 16 inch laced wheel and Avon tire. The rest of the pieces are relics from back-in-the-day. Note the sissy bar, the AMF Sporty tank, and the Pabst Blue Ribbon shift knob.

It might be 2006 on your calendar, but in Rod's garage it's still 1972.

Rod Grimme's Chopper is a throwback to 1972, carefully assembled from genuine Harley-Davidson parts or old aftermarket parts. The old Sportster tank was left with factory paint.

When Rod decides to shift he just puts his boot on the clutch pedal and grabs 'hold of the tapper handle.

Rod's V-twin is a real Panhead with aftermarket covers. Damaged cases and heads had to be repaired as part of the restoration process.

Chapter Eight

'57 Panhead Basket Build

Start with a Pile of Parts

IN THE BEGINNING

For building a bike in the true spirit of old skool, nothing beats an old 45, Knuck, Pan or Shovel. These vintage bikes have the old-skool class that anyone can appreciate. This particular bike started as a basket case Panhead that was picked up for under $8,000.00. The bike was classified as a "basket" because all the pieces and parts of the bike were mostly disassembled, and the bike was brought home in a number of boxes and baskets of

The finished product, a cool, low-dollar basket-case rescued from extinction and garage-built to what you see above. The stroked Panhead motor is housed in a Santee frame with a lot of fabricated parts.

parts. When you purchase a vintage basket case it is important to look over all the components to be sure they are all from the same bike. Be sure any engine or frame numbers are in good, non-tampered-with, condition. Check that all the individual parts, such as the cases and heads, are in good shape and don't need extensive repairs.

Depending on your resources, and welding-machining capabilities, almost anything can be fixed. Companies like Solutions Machining and Welding specialize in repairing busted up parts and putting them back together. I have seen many nasty bikes and bike components that I thought for sure couldn't be repaired, but Weyland from Solutions is one of the best and has always come through.

Unfortunately, many basket cases are bits and pieces from various bikes and various years. If you're looking for a true, accurate, vintage restoration, check the parts carefully to be sure you are getting what you really want. Also, check the paperwork to see if there is a free and clear original title with the parts, or will you need to register the bike as "special construction." Bikes with clean original titles always will bring more money on the market as it is getting harder and harder to find complete basket case projects with all the parts from the same original bike. After going through all the

I was pretty excited the day the basket-Pan came home. I could already envision the finished product in my head, as it would look rolling down the road.

After a few hours of scrounging through the boxes I assembled the parts into a roller, just to get a feel for the bike and evaluate what would be needed to finish the project.

miscellaneous parts, I recommend you write down any and all information on the parts, and get the VIN numbers to check with the DMV. In this way you know the engine and/or frame are not registered as a stolen bike. This would end your dream build real fast, if after assembly the DMV confiscates your new ride. Always be 100% sure everything is legal before you spend your hard earned money!

Pictured nearby is the Panhead the day I brought it

The Panhead build inspired a new wave of thinking about motivating kids. I finally found a way to get the kids excited about coming to school.

home. I quickly took the parts and assembled a mock up roller to get a feel for the bike and to help me determine what other components would be needed. To mock up the bike, you don't worry about loctite or correct torque specifications as the bike will be completely disassembled again.

One important aspect that needs to be considered is the garage or shop where the assembly will take place. At the time I bought this project it was the middle of winter and I did not have a heated garage. This quickly ended my hopes of working on the bike at home when I had free time. The extreme cold Minnesota winter had me looking for a new place to continue the build. I am a teacher in a well equipped shop, and I had been working on my old iron head Sportster at that school shop with a great amount of excitement from the kids, so I knew this could be a cool class project. After talking to the students and the administration I brought the bike into my classroom for our first basket case Chopper building class project. Chopper class with Mr. Baas was officially formed, and our high school shop class would never be the same.

The motor needed some TLC which included repairing stripped rocker cover screw holes in the heads. These are common faults in old Panheads and can be repaired with the right equipment.

STEP ONE

After going through and cleaning up all the parts, the best thing to do is create a list of everything you need to accomplish to finish the build, with all the needed parts prioritized on an inventory sheet. This will help you to keep the process organized and allow you to order any needed parts in advance so you are not stuck waiting on something, or missing key components at the end of the build. There is nothing worse than wasting days or weeks waiting on last-minute parts that you forgot. This is where some of the vintage parts catalogs or trained motorcycle mechanics will be useful. Catalogs like V-Twin, J&P Vintage, Superior Motorcycles, Kustomwerks and Jammer Cycle products can help you to locate and order any needed parts.

REFERENCES

A good manual for the bike you are building is also a must. You will get many important tech tips and build diagrams to help you sort out what goes where, and what you may need to complete the build. Torque specifications, and assembly and disassembly sequences, will aid you in your build when you have trouble. There are a wide variety of manuals available and I always like to get the original Harley-Davidson publication as well as some others from companies such as Clymer. The more references the better, I have found that some manuals have different pictures and reference information that can help greatly. If your bike is a mix of parts, just buy the manual that's as close as possible to your particular machine.

BUILD OUTLINE

The most important aspect of the construction, especially to the novice builder, is to break the build up into three detailed sections: the front, the middle, and the rear. This will help to better organize what you need to get done on each area, and also create a detailed list that you can check off as you get things done. Organization is a great tool to use which will not only help you in your build but make it easier to ask for assistance when needed in certain areas. Time is money, so you definitely don't want to waste extra time with a bike shop - trying to figure out where you are or what you're trying to accomplish.

The front end includes: the fork assembly, neck cups and bearings, risers, bars, controls, headlight, front brake, front fender, axle, wheel and tire. The mid section may include the gas tank, speedometer, ignition switch, wiring/circuit breakers, kick stand, controls, motor, transmission, oil tank, battery box and battery, carburetor, air cleaner, coils, seat, voltage regulator, rotor, stator, and primary system.

The rear section may include the rear wheel and tire, sprocket, rear breaks, license plate holder, tail light, rear fender, rear axle, and fender struts. Some items may vary depending on the year and model of the bike you are building. This is where a

My inspiration, Pa Baas, working on the final assembly of the stroked Panhead motor. Without his guidance and support, this bike would not be where it is today.

Expert TIG welder, and good friend, Dan Davis teaching me the correct way to repair the stripped rocker cover holes.

An original 4-speed tranny with a ratchet top.

The adjustable tranny plate that was needed to install the 4-speed into the frame.

motorcycle mechanic can help out greatly. After this list is created you can prioritize and create a game plan for the build.

BASKET CASE COMPONENT EVALUATION

After I completed my outline, and organized everything for the build, I started evaluating the condition of the Panhead motor, the transmission and other components, so I could make any necessary repairs or replacements. The motor for this build is a 1957 FLH Pan, with jugs punched out and ready for the .060 inch-over S&S pistons. Be aware that when the cylinders are punched out .060 inch they will not have room for any future rebuilds, unless you get them sleeved. Otherwise plan on buying a new set of cylinders for the next major rebuild.

Other non-stock parts used on this motor included an Andrews "B" grind cam, solid lifters, oversized valves, S&S oil pump and carburetor, and S&S 4-1/2 inch stroker flywheels. This is far from a stock rebuild, so if you're a true vintage collector looking for stock parts this would not be the type of basket case project for you, unless you have the means to change everything back to stock.

This Panhead does utilize the original cases, jugs and 1948 heads, so I wanted to be sure they were all in good shape. The extra power and torque will put extra stress on the old metal and if there are any major flaws, they will crack. Luckily, if your basket has any major problems with any of those components you can buy new aftermarket pieces that can be interchanged with the stock parts which are of very high quality. As mentioned in Chapter Five, a variety of firms make quality aftermarket parts for old motors, going all the way back to the Flathead and Knucklehead.

MOTOR REPAIR AND ASSEMBLY

After the engine parts were inspected and repaired, and ready to be reassembled, the inventory outline sheet was double checked. Then the motor reassembly could begin. I purchased new gaskets and seals for the entire motor. New gaskets always should be used with any motor assembly to ensure the finished product is solid and leak-free. The new pistons were slipped into the jugs, and then my father stepped in to correctly assemble and shim the gears in the cam cover.

Anything assembled improperly at this stage of the build will only come back and haunt you down the road when the bike breaks. This is another reason having all the proper reference manuals and skilled help is so important. Make sure you get a qualified person for any engine work you can't do yourself, and never trust a novice with such an important task!

After the entire motor was gone through and assembled up to the heads, we found the heads had some stripped threads and worn out heli coils on the top where the covers bolt on. This is a common problem on vintage Panheads as people often over tightened the covers to try and fix leaks, which only results in stripped threads and more leads. To fix these you must TIG weld up the holes and then remark, drill and tap new holes.

This was a fairly tedious process but with the help of an experienced TIG welder the task was correctly done in a couple of hours. The following pictures show our head repair. To start with we ground out the stripped areas to ensure good pene-

Progress on the Pan project. The motor and tranny are connected by the BDL belt drive system.

There is nothing cooler than the look of an old Panhead. At this point of the build I was getting very excited to get the project completed and on the road.

With the sheet metal in place, and the oil bag finally mounted, the bike's stance was apparent. The clean bare bones look was coming together nicely.

The Pan motor and 4-speed tranny connected with a BDL belt drive and a 5-finger clutch assembly.

tration and a solid weld. Once the clean up was finished we then were able to weld up each hole and resurface the gasket surface. Finally, we were able to carefully drill and tap new holes for the classic Panhead rocker covers.

TRANSMISSION

Once the motor was completely finished, we started on the transmission. The transmission top cover was removed to inspect the gears and shifting fingers to be sure everything was good to go. Now is the time you want to replace any bad parts, breaking down 500 miles into a trip is a real bummer. Check all wear on the components, and check for play in any bearings to be sure they do not need replacing. I was fortunate with this transmission; everything was in great shape internally and nothing had to be replaced. I did replace the seals on the main shaft just to be safe and avoid any leaking, but otherwise it was ready to run.

With the older style transmissions an adjustable tranny plate is needed which allows for the transmission to be adjusted for proper alignment and tension. The transmission used on this bike is the original Harley-Davidson 4 speed with the hand-shift jockey lid. I am running this bike with a suicide shift set up which is a definitely more dangerous and a bit more challenging to operate than the ratchet top style transmission with foot shift. The jockey lid was made to be run with a tank shift utilizing a shifting gate that allowed you to hit each gear by putting the lever into the appropriate gate.

When run as a suicide set up, shifting directly off the cover, you need to learn the feel for each gear. An inexperienced rider will find it very easy to miss gears, as you can push the lever from first gear all the way through and past second, third, and fourth gear in one inaccurate shift. Again, it should be noted that a novice rider is not encouraged to try suicide shifting.

Grinding the frame in preparation for a custom seat Pan. Paul Cox would be covering the seat pan at a later date. Because the pan sits directly on the frame rails, some minor grinding was needed to be sure it would sit flat.

THE MOCK-UP

After getting the motor and transmission completely finished and ready to install into the frame, I set them aside until the frame was ready. I then inspected the frame for any repairs it might need and made sure all mounting points and threads were true and in good shape. Next, I installed the front end, risers and handle bars, rear fender, and wheels to have what is called a rolling chassis. This is where the bike starts to take shape. At this point you get to see how the bike will look. Don't let the excitement to get it done override your common sense. Take your time and do it right.

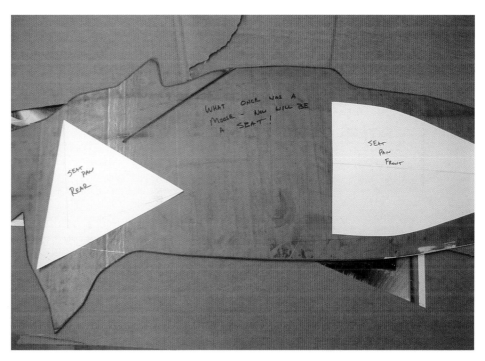

The custom seat pan started as a paper template of the shape, and a piece of scrap 1/8 inch steel.

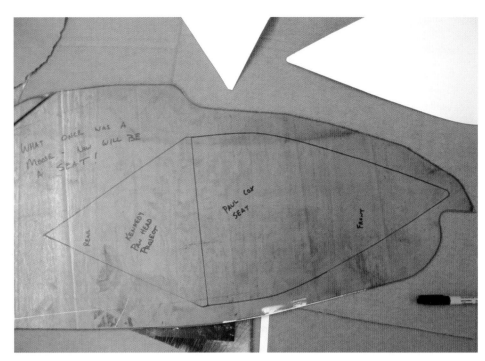

Once the template design was transferred to the steel, the Pan could be cut out.

Proper alignment of the front and rear wheels is very important. To do this you must get the wheels centered in the frame. I use a string, run down the center of the front tire, the neck, along the top center of the backbone and down the center of the rear wheel. After you have the line straight down and the wheels have been adjusted to dead center, you then take a caliper and take measurements from the hub bearing to the inside of the frame or fork. A steel spacer is then machined to fit over the axle and fill the gaps so the front and rear axle can be tightened, and the wheels will be secured in the center of the frame. Double check your alignment after the axles are tightened by running a straight line again down the center of the frame and over the tires, they should be centered within the frame.

Be sure your wheels spin freely and do not bind when the axle nuts are tightened. If they do bind, you must go back through and re-check the spacers, incorrectly machined spacers can cause the bearings to bind which will lock up the wheel and damage the bearing. Also, don't forget to allow for any space taken up by brake caliper carriers, which will require some additional calculation and machining to get the spacers correct. New spacer kits can be purchased in various lengths, but if you are able

The cut seat pan bent to fit the frame. After the pan's rear section gets rolled to match the radius of the fender, the seat will sit snug to the frame and fender.

to make your own it will save you money and give you the satisfaction of knowing you did it yourself. Take your time and do not rush any aspect of the build. Always double check any work you have done. The right way is the best way even if it takes longer than you planned.

After the rolling chassis was mocked up, the motor and tranny could then be placed in the frame for alignment and shimming. The motor and tranny should not be bolted down tight at this point. Make sure the points where the motor and tranny sit on the frame (frame pads) are clean of any paint or debris, you want bare metal here or you will not get accurate readings for your shims. Once the engine and transmission are loosely bolted into the frame, the next step of alignment can begin.

PRIMARY DRIVE

Primary choices include the enclosed chain or belt drive. Although I do like the traditional enclosed primary look, I chose to run a BDL 3 inch open primary drive for a more industrial hard-core appearance. This set up, used on the older four speed transmissions, does not use an inner support plate to align the motor and transmission like a newer style primary system does. The heavy-duty cases used on old transmissions allow for this without any real danger of failure. Newer style transmissions are not made

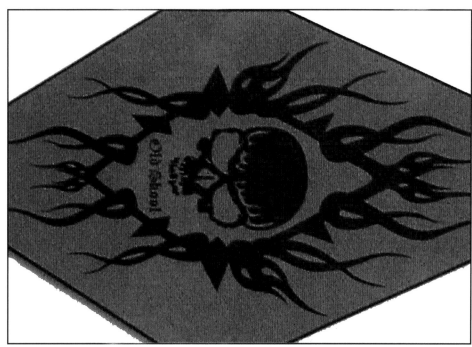

After the seat pan was finished I worked on the design that Paul Cox would tool into the leather - with help from Amy, my graphic-designer wife. We created this full-color, full-size print of what we wanted on the seat. This was then sent to Gasoline Alley for Paul to use as he created our seat cover.

The finished product is simply amazing and a true work of art. Paul tooled the design exactly as we requested, there is no doubt he is one of the best!

The custom Baas Metal Craft remote oil filter bracket that was used on the Panhead project. This custom piece is one of the little details that make a bike truly unique.

to withstand such abuse and should always be used with the inner primary support. To align the motor and transmission on this style a little more time needs to be taken to ensure it is done properly.

With the transmission mounting plate installed in the frame and the transmission loosely set on the plate, install the belt pulleys and belt. You can then use a straight edge and align the rear pulley with the front motor pulley, then be sure the rear chain sprockets are in proper alignment as well. Once the alignment is correct, carefully bolt the engine to the frame securely with the proper manufacturer-supplied torque specifications. Then double check the belt pulley alignment again, and tighten the transmission down with the belt being fairly tight.

Once the motor and transmission are secured, you can then set the proper belt tension using the transmission adjuster screw. Be sure to use loctite and grade 8 Nylock nuts and bolts on all these areas as vibration will quickly loosen and misalign parts not secured properly. You can then kick over the bike and check the tracking of the belt. The belt should not drift off the pulleys, and should stay straight and true in relation to the edges of the front and rear pulley. Any misalignment will be apparent at this point and should be fixed before you move on.

A nice side shot showing the finished Paul Cox seat, and the remote oil filter assembly in place.

After this was accomplished the clutch lever was attached and the oil tank could then be installed. With the major mock up complete we could focus on all the smaller items on our list that needed to be done to complete the mock up.

SEAT

There are many cool old-skool seats for sale through the various manufacturers but nothing beats the look of a one-of-a-kind custom made seat. For the seat on this bike we were fortunate to have the best leather working wizard on the planet. Paul Cox created a hand-tooled master-piece for the bike that truly is a functional work of art.

We decided not to use the traditional spring seat that so many run, and go for a hardcore, slammed-to-the-frame-seat. This style seat with a rigid frame is not something you'd want to try if you have back problems or are looking for a soft Cadillac-style comfortable ride. To me, the clean, hard-core look makes it all worthwhile. I have ridden it, and yes the back and kidneys take a beating. But if I wanted extreme comfort I'd sell my Panhead and buy a Road King. Paul uses the best materials in his seats and I have been 100% happy with not only the look but also the quality of the seat.

A picture of the installed Chopper wiring kit supplied by Bitter-End Choppers.

Here's the custom seat pan at an earlier stage in the bike-building process. Note how we rolled the back of the pan to match the radius of the rear fender. At this point the bike was really turning into a cool old-skool ride.

To begin prepping the frame for the custom seat, first the backbone of the frame needed to be cut and ground down to allow the seat pan to sit flush. A cardboard template of the seat was then cut to make sure the new seat would fit the frame properly. Once the template is finished, you can cut out and trace the template onto steel or aluminum to be cut by hand. If you have access to CNC equipment,however, the seat pan dimensions can be created in a CAD/CAM program and then sent to the CNC machine to be cut, which is what we did with this seat pan. The exact dimensions were created, and the pan was cut perfectly with minimal clean up needed at the edges.

Once the seat Pan is cut it must be bent, formed, and welded to the exact shape needed to fit the frame snugly. To bend the radius to follow the rear fender, you can bend it by hand, slowly checking your progress to be sure it fits, or use a ring roller which creates a nice smooth curve in the steel that is easily adjusted to get the exact radius you need.

After the seat is completed and fits the frame the way you want, solid mounting points should be added to the pan to limit the possibility of someone walking off with your seat or it falling off the bike when you are not sitting on it.

The seat pan should be painted or plated if it is carbon steel to eliminate any rusting problems. If it is made from stainless steel or aluminum then it can be left bare if you choose. The pan can then be sent out for the final step - padding and leather covering.

The possible seat design for a custom-tooled seat is almost endless, and this is a great way to really add that unique touch to a Bobber. Your seat can be a one-off design that no one else has. My wife created the unique old-skool design that was sent to Paul to be tooled into the seat. As you can see, from the initial design to the finished product, Paul made it exactly the way we wanted and I was blown away at the high quality tooling he achieved on the leather. The work was flawless!

OIL FILTER TRIBUTE

As a tribute to Indian Larry and Paul Cox, whose bikes are timeless works of art, and who were the first ones to show their support of my dream for high school bike building, all the bikes we build utilize the Fram HP1 remote oil filter assembly seen on many of their bikes. This set up gives the bike the big beefy Ford truck filter look, using the high-flow-low-restriction HP1 race filter. Complete kits with custom fabricated brackets are available through Baas Metal Craft or the filter bracket with license plate mount is available through Indian-Larry.com.

For this build I decided to make a personalized bracket, which has the same

The custom machined brass foot pegs we made for the build. All the bikes we build get a pair of these unique pegs.

flame design as the seat and the words "FTF" and "57 PAN" cut into it. The custom bracket was aligned and welded to the frame - which should be done after you know what taillight style you will use. In our case, we planned to run a side mount plate and didn't want the filter assembly to interfere with that, or have it too close which would make it difficult to change filters. Be aware that you need access to your axle adjusters as well.

Once the bracket is welded to the frame, and the filter housing bolted to the bracket, the custom oil lines can be attached. It is very important that the oil lines are hooked up correctly on this set up or you will starve your motor of oil and blow it up. The filter system should be on the return side of the oil pump. This means that the oil coming out of the motor should be routed to flow into the "IN" side of the filter housing. The oil line on the "OUT" side of the filter housing should be routed back into the oil tank. Then from the oil tank, the line runs in the standard configuration - feeding the oil pump with the clean filtered oil from the tank. Spin on the filter before you attach the oil lines. Once the system is completed, you have a race inspired industrial looking touch to your bike.

Little details like the eyeball on the axle adjuster, and the hot rod style wrapped pipes, help to set this bike apart from the rest.

The final assembly of the Panhead, with help from student Clark Davis, consisted of double checking everything on the bike. Things like drivetrain alignment, and all the fasteners to be sure they were tightened to the correct torque specifications.

WIRING

Once the bike is assembled to this point, and before the sheet metal is attached, I like to get all the wiring figured out. This Panhead was using the stock-style circuit breaker, which has one line running off of it. There are no blinkers, or digital gauges, so the wiring is very simple. I picked up one of the Bitter End - Old School Choppers, Inc. basic Chopper wiring diagrams. This kit un-complicates things by leaving out all the crap that many garage built old-skool Choppers don't need any way: turn signals, speedometer, radio, horn, bells, whistles, and all the rest. This kit comes with a detailed diagram and all needed supplies.

This wiring system covers circuit breakers, starter relay, starter, alternator, ignition, regulator/rectifier, kill switch/lock, headlight, taillight, brake lights, battery, only the bare essentials. This kit let's you get wired fast so you can make the big run, yet serves as a basis for later add-ons (not covered here). This kit includes color-coded schematics to make drawings easy to read and the wires easy to trace. The wire colors match stock (where possible) to make matching up to electrical components (such as headlights/taillights) simpler.

Designed for ground-up Chopper wiring, this kit does not include a big wiring harness, which helps to save you big bucks. Basic instructions and a pointer sheet are included, as well as complete tech support via phone or e-mail. This is one of the best ways for the garage builder to do it himself and get through the mess of wiring. Big Daddy Al can be contacted at the phone number or web site listed in the back of this book.

GAS TANK

Initially, the tank we used was an aftermarket Fat-Bob style tank. This gave the bike plenty of gas for the long runs and also has a big beefy look to it. We mounted the tanks using aftermarket weld-on tank brackets and hardware. The mounts were tack-welded on first, then the tank was installed and checked for proper alignment before being finish welded. Once the tank mounting was finished, the tank was taken off and given a rattle can, flat black paint job. I like to run this style paint initially on my bikes because if any modifications or changes are needed you don't run the risk of destroying an expensive paint job. Always remember to pressure test and seal any tank you use to avoid leaks, which will ruin your paint job real fast! We used an aftermarket dash to house the ignition switch and the speedometer, all of which are available through any good parts supplier.

CONTROLS

Hand and foot controls vary greatly in terms of both style and quality. What you use will depend on the other components you use and the style of the bike. Since this bike was to be run with a suicide shift there was no need for a hand clutch, and a foot clutch lever system needed to be attached. To do this I fabricated a brass pull lever, which I attached to my forward control, then the pull

After double-checking the entire bike, it was ready to be taken off the lift and given a test run.

lever to the release arm of the four-speed tranny. Be sure the system pulls straight and true without any binding, especially with a brass pull rod like this because any binding or side flex will result in a broken arm. Foot pegs and brake/clutch pegs were designed and machined and then attached to the controls.

These pegs I custom made from brass and they really add a unique touch. Since brass fittings and other odds and ends were going to be used, these brass pegs fit in well with the look of the bike. To make the pegs I started by measuring a set of stock pegs and then determined the size I wanted for the custom ones.

I picked up some 1-1/2 inch, solid brass bar stock and began machining the pegs on my lathe. After they were completed and installed I was very

The initial test run of the Panhead project. All ran well, and with some minor adjustments the bike became one of the most reliable bikes I've ever owned. The bike is now my main transportation. Every summer I take an annual 1,000 mile trip with my Dad, Uncle Dean, and Cousins Grim, Rod and Jesse.

happy with the way they looked. These pegs are something that no catalog offers. It is important to remember that sometimes you may find after you have put a component or custom piece on the bike, it might not fit the look. Don't be afraid to start over with different ideas and designs. Build a bike you can be one-hundred percent happy with.

BRAKES

The next task I worked on was the installation of all the brake lines. This bike utilizes aftermarket GMA disc brakes front and rear, which have more stopping

After the bike was finished, I went back and made a few changes, which include the spiderweb fender struts seen here. Strut designs are limitless and almost anything is possible.

power than the traditional drum. These types of brakes need to be bled properly after installation to ensure proper stopping power when you take the bike on the road. To bleed the hydraulic brake lines, first fill the brake reservoir with DOT 5 fluid and pump the lever or pedal. Add fluid as necessary until the lines are full. Then with the help of a friend pump the brake pedal/lever until you feel the pressure build up. Then hold the pedal/lever down while the bleeder screw is cracked open to allow the fluid and trapped air to squirt out. Have a rag handy as this is a messy process. Repeat this process until there is no more air in the lines or calipers.

The rear brake caliper may need to be removed and bled off the rotor, if the caliper mounts so the bleeder is on the bottom side of the caliper (any air in the caliper is trapped at the "top," and can't be bled off unless the bleeder is at the top as well). Clean up all brake fluid and test the brakes. Repeat the process if necessary or if you notice the brakes getting squishy. Don't forget to use some brake cleaner and spray down the caliper and pads to remove any fluid that may be left - which would result in poor stopping power.

FINAL ASSEMBLY

Once everything has been double checked and secured with Loctite and all adjustments are finished, add the proper amount of oil to the motor and transmission per the manufacturers specifications. Now it's time to add gas and start the bike. If you are running a new motor or a freshly rebuilt one let the motor warm up and after the first couple of rides re-torque the head bolts. The pushrods should also be checked to be sure they are still at proper adjustment, and any leaks should be addressed. It's a good idea to check all the nuts and bolts on the bike after the first ride or two. I like to ride close to home or with a chase vehicle for my first ride, because nine times out of ten, something will go wrong on the test run and then I'm stranded on the side of the road.

MODIFICATIONS

Pictured on the preceding page is the bike after it was completed and road ready. I ran the Panhead this way for one year and then decided to change the look a little. Since the Fat Bob gas tanks were from the aftermarket I had no problem taking them off and installing a smaller Sportster tank. I like the look of this tank, mounted high on the backbone. It has more of the Frisco style and puts the Panhead motor out in the open more, which makes it become the focal point of the bike.

The Fat Bobs sat so low over the heads it almost hid some of the beauty of the old Panhead. At the same time I blacked out the lower legs of the front end and added black fork boots from Jammer to give the bike more of the rat rod, retro look. The rear fender was cut down shorter, or bobbed, and custom spider web fender struts were created with my CNC plasma cutting machine. I used the same machine to cut out a brass knuckle cut out that I TIG

After running the Panhead for one summer I decided to make some changes. The Fat Bobs were taken off and the peanut tank installed, with paint work by Hering Kustoms. The bars and risers were also added, and the front end was blackened out with some rattle can flat black and fork gaiters.

welded to the fender as a mini sissy bar. The gas tank received a retro satin black pinstriped paint job from Hering Kustoms The old hot rod Von Dutch style pin striping is a very popular, yet classic way to have your bike painted. The drag bars and stock risers were traded out for a set of dog bone risers and Z-bars. Overall the bike has a unique look that blends old vintage style with some new technology and really stands out from the sea of Choppers that I see on the streets.

BACK TO THE ORIGINAL

The next changes this bike will be getting include putting the motor and transmission back into the original straight-leg rigid Harley-Davidson frame. For rolling chassis purposes a wide glide front end was used, but has since been swapped out for an original Harley inline Springer. Along with the original vintage Harley Springer front end, star hub wheels front and rear with mechanical rear drum breaks will be used to give it that classic true old-skool style. This will move the bike closer to the original, bare bones, retro styling that I really like.

The addition of an antique Pabst Blue Ribbon tapper handle, a cool bar-end mirror from Goblin Millworks, and the Baas Metal Craft fork brace, all add to the bike's unique look.

Although drum brakes are not the best as far as true stopping power, they are definitely a true old skool addition to any bike. The frame was a victim of the Chopper days and someone cut off the toolbox mount, sidecar loops, floorboard tabs as well as the original tank mounts. The original style toolbox was put back on as well as the floorboards, and the sidecar loops will be replaced to bring the frame back to the stock look. This frame is a '57, which is the last year of the straight leg rigid so it is worth some money, as many of them did not survive the Chopper days. The final goal will be to build the bike back to its true original FLH dresser look, but that will be quite a while down the road.

The bare bones garage built qualities of this bike make it a true vintage custom classic. The mixture of the vintage power plant, swap meet parts as well as the many custom one-off pieces keep this bike from looking like so many others lined up at bike events.

Chapter Nine

Build Number Two

Donations are a Good Thing

After the Panhead build (Chapter Eight) was finished we received a lot of press on what was happening in the class with the students. This allowed me to take the program to the next level - a fund-raiser Bobber project bike that could be

sold after completion to help support the shop classes I teach. This started what would be the first in a series of high school builds done by the students relying entirely on donated parts. This idea is not only great for the kids, but the entire bike

This bike was built by my high school students in my Chopper class in under 2 months, from all donated parts. Any pieces we needed which were not donated we fabricated in class with no outside help.

is packed into a frame that is also about 20 pounds lighter than a stock rigid, straight-leg or wishbone frame. This high-quality Spartan frame utilized a single Ford-radius-rod, gooseneck, down tube. No clean up was needed at all for the frame and it came ready for the bike assembly with beautifully TIG-welded seams. An added bonus of this Spartan frame is that before any tube is bent, the design is created in Auto CAD to check the rake,

The Spartan Frame shortly after delivery. Spartan frames are high quality and have many options to fit your perfect custom building dreams.

industry. Getting young minds involved in a project like this is a great way to create some excitement about school. It also helps the students pick up many skills that will make them better prepared for the real world.

SPARTAN DONATES THE FOUNDATION

We had an idea of the style of bike we wanted to build, but were going to have to take what we could get from donations to get the bike done. We wanted a low, sleek-looking bike with an oldskool, retro board-track style, mated with some new technology. George Counes, from Spartan Frameworks, quickly answered our prayers by donating a custom hand-made frame and Springer fork. The frame is Spartans "Killed by Death" model with a 33-degree rake, four inches of stretch in the top tube and none in the downtube. The Springer is a Spartan 1-inch over T-Bone model. This laid the foundation for exactly what we were looking to build. Spartan frames are constructed of 4130-alloy steel (normalized), which makes for a tough and durable chrome molly chassis. These frames are designed and tested to take the abuse of everyday hard riding, burnouts, wheelies, and racing on any type of road. All that

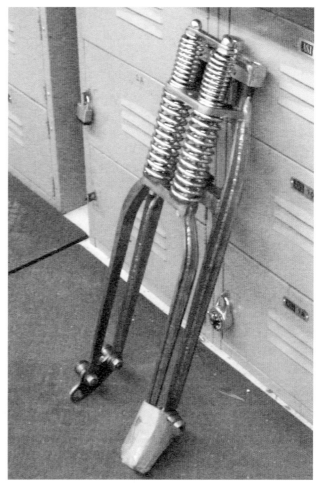

The T-bone Spartan Springer, another one of George Counes' awesome creations.

The adjustable tranny plate we used from Hank Young. This allows for quick and easy alignment of your transmission in custom frames.

stretch, trail, ground clearance, and wheel base, which will ensure that you get the exact frame you want.

Then there was George's T-Bone Springer front end. Wow is all I could say! This Springer was a unique and amazing addition that truly makes the bike stand out. All Spartan Springers are created and sold with a chromed top clamp, crown nut, and top nut, and all that is needed to install the fork is a set of bearings and dust shields. These Springers are constructed of cold rolled steel and are 100% TIG welded with superior weld quality. They can be made to order at any length, width and for any custom applications you may have. The Springers retail for around $1950.00 and also are backed by a lifetime guarantee.

TOOLS AND EQUIPMENT

Once the frame and front end were delivered to the school, we began seeking out all the other components we needed to make the bike a rolling chassis. After all the components were secured we began to mock up the bike. Before you begin the mock-up, be sure you have adequate space and the proper tools for the assembly. Air and power tools will be needed as well as a complete set of hand tools to properly assemble the bike. A quality bike lift will help any builder to raise and lower the bike as needed during

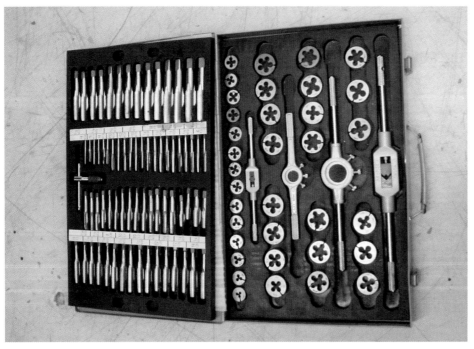

From taping holes in fender struts, to cleaning out the threads in the frame after painting, a set of taps and dies is one of the handiest tools you will every buy.

certain stages of the process. Although I have built bikes entirely on the ground, after I purchased my first lift I immediately saw how important a lift can be. No more awkward positions, or lying on my back to get at the low areas of the bike. The lift made everything 100 times easier. An air compressor with a variety of air tools such as an impact wrench, grinders, and cut off tools should be on hand if possible. If you do not have air tools or a compressor, many power tools can be purchased in electric models as well. A good drill and drill set should always be close by in any bike shop, as well as a tap and die set. You need a basic mechanic's tool set which includes wrenches, files, Allen set, metal shears, torx bit set, ratchet and socket sets, pliers, screwdrivers, adjustable wrenches, vise grips, hammers, tape measure, and a torque wrench.

Also needed will be an electrical kit with various items such as wire in different gauges and colors, heat shrink-wrap, electrical connectors, wire cutter, wire stripper, and a crimping tool. If you will be doing the fabrication of spacers and other parts yourself, a lathe and mill are a must as well as is a good quality caliper for taking precise measurements for the different pieces that will need to be machined. A good quality MIG or TIG welder is needed as well for various steps in

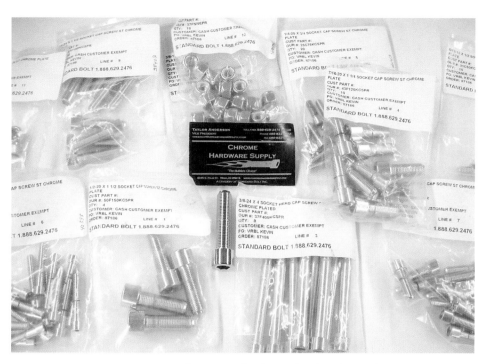

Always use high quality hardware for your build, from a reputable company like Chrome Hardware Supply. If you use cheap hardware, failure will occur which can cause damage to your bike or severe bodily injury.

A welder may not be essential, but it sure is handy. TIG welders are quite expensive, though a small to medium sized MIG is fairly affordable.

In addition to hand tools, you're going to need power tools like those shown. If you don't have an air compressor, you can even buy electric impact wrenches.

A good quality lift is also a great help in any build. Though there are other brands, we use Handy lifts in our classroom.

construction, if custom pieces are going to be used. Always remember that you can never have enough tools. The more tools the better, if you do not have a complete set you will find yourself making numerous trips to the store to buy the pieces you need to complete certain steps of the build.

BUILD HARDWARE

Using the proper hardware is also a must in any bike build. We were lucky to have Chrome Hardware Supply on hand to donate all the chrome hardware we needed to bolt the bike together. Chrome Hardware Supply is the quality leader for chrome and polished fasteners. All of their chrome hardware is baked after plating, which is essential to maintaining the strength and integrity of the part. There are suppliers who don't take this extra step, which can result in failure under stress. All of the chrome screws and bolts they supply are made from Grade 8 steel, providing superior performance over grade 5 fasteners. Their dedication to quality has been apparent from the start of their company. They started their business supplying fasteners for helicopters and military aircraft, the space shuttle, and satellites, submarines, and other critical applications. They know the importance of quality.

MOCK UP

The first thing to do when beginning a mock up is to install the front end and wheels. Wheels and tires for our project were donated by Ghostriders of Lakeville, Minnesota. A 16 inch rim and a 130 tire combination was used on the rear, and for the front a 21 inch rim and tire were installed. The plan was to eventually run an Avon gangster white wall in the rear and an Avon speed master in the front, which would give the bike a bit of that vintage feel in the rubber.

While the new tires were on order we used a set of old rubber in the same size for mock up purposes. Once the tires were mounted and the wheels were in place, alignment could begin. Wheel alignment is very important on any bike you build to ensure safe, trouble-free operation of the bike when you are riding down the road. Start by finding the center of the bike and the rear wheel. Once you have established that the wheels are centered in the middle of the frame, measurements can be taken for axle spacers. The axle spacers can then be bought through the various part suppliers, or machined in house if you have access to a lathe. We used solid bar stock to begin with and drilled the 3/4 inch hole for the axle. We then marked our measurements on the bar and cut them to size. Once all the spacers were created we installed them on the axles and tightened the bolts to factory specifications.

The custom made bars that were created using a set of old drag bars. We cut them up and re-welded them to fit the style of the bike. The low-slung board track style was apparent in this set.

The sleek low lines of the bike really started to take shape quickly in the mock-up stage. Make sure all potential problems are addressed at this stage to eliminate any major problems during final assembly.

An adjustable tranny plate will be needed to properly install the transmission. Do your research before purchasing your components to make sure they will mate up with your frame. These 5-speed Softail trannies are very popular and can be picked up fairly cheaply.

A kicker definitely adds an old-skool touch to any bike. Kickers were the starting devices used for many years before the birth of the electric start.

Double check your alignment and be sure the wheels spin freely and do not bind. Depending on the brake system you use, be sure to compensate for any caliper brackets that the axle runs through. PM supplied the rear brakes and rotor for this build. After the wheels were secured and checked we then installed the forward controls and kick stand, compliments of Jammer Cycle Products.

HANDLEBARS

The handlebars were fabricated by the students in class from old bars that were cut and re-welded to fit the shape needed. These bars were created to have a low, board-track style with an internal throttle from Exile Cycles and no clutch lever. This gives the bars a clean dropped down, bare-bones vintage look. When fabricating your own set of bars it is important, for safety reasons, to always join the two bar pieces together at 30 degree angles and use slugs inside the bar material as well as rosettes to secure the two pieces together. Rosettes are where you have holes drilled through the bar material, exposing the internal slug. This gives you access to weld the slug to the bars, which adds a great deal of strength to the design.

Once the bars were welded up, they were ground smooth and then wrapped in black hockey tape. This allowed us to finally roll the bike off the lift to get a good look at its stance on the ground. We were very happy with the sleek low look and ready to continue the mock up. The sleek low lines of the bike became apparent at this point and the stance of this bike was exactly what we were looking for.

MOTOR & DRIVETRAIN

This bike utilized a stock Harley five-speed transmission that was donated by Lucky's Garage in Minneapolis, MN. A RevTech kicker kit was installed on the transmission compliments of Kokesh Motorcycle, of Spring Lake Park, Minnesota. When building a bike with a retro look, a kicker is definitely an old-skool touch that is a must. We then used one of Hank Young's adjustable transmission plates, which allowed easy and accurate alignment of the transmission in the frame. S&S helped sponsor this build with their generous donation of the new 88-inch Evolution-style motor.

Originally we planned to use an old Shovelhead motor, so when the new motor was donated a slight modification of the frame was necessary. The modification became necessary because the donated Evo-style motor is taller than a Shovel. We had to notch the frame's backbone to make room for the bigger motor. To do this we trimmed away part of the frame tubing, to allow for proper clearance, and welded a new recessed

S&S helped us a great deal by donating the new 88-inch Evolution style motor.

The frame was designed to fit a Shovelhead, we needed to make some adjustments so the taller Evo would fit. The students cut out sections of frame tubing and welded in concave pieces that allow the motor to clear. By adding the concave sections there was no loss of strength in the frame.

Alignment of the motor and tranny is fairly easy to do with the use of the inner primary. After this is bolted on securely, the fit of the transmission should be checked as noted in the nearby text.

After the shimming was completed, and the transmission and motor were properly torqued down, the belt was installed. Always check the tracking of your belt to be sure that everything is lined up correctly.

piece of steel into the void.

After a small amount of grinding, the modification was complete. Next, the motor and tranny were loosely set in place, and the charging system, compliments of Spyke, could be installed per manufacturer's recommendations. Finally, we used the BDL 3 inch open belt drive primary, also donated to the project, to finish off the drivetrain assembly. After the inner primary plate was secured to the engine and transmission, the alignment of the engine and transmission on their mounting pads could be checked.

Be aware, the driveline shimming/alignment process is very important, if you don't shim the motor and transmission properly undue stress will occur and broken motor and transmission mounts can happen. For more on this topic, see the Alignment Sequence in Chapter Ten). After the alignment is double-checked and all shimming is completed the motor and transmission can be secured to the frame tightly with the proper Grade 8 bolts. Be sure to lock nuts to proper specifications. The belt was checked one last time for proper tracking and we then took the inner primary off to be sure it would go on and off smoothly. If it binds at all, there is an alignment problem and the motor and tranny will need to be re shimmed to eliminate the problem.

GAS TANK

Once all these parts were assembled and lined up properly we tackled some of the other aspects of the build. The students hand-crafted the custom gas tank entirely in class, with no expensive English wheel or planishing hammer. If they could do it so can you!

For the tank the students started by creating a paper template of the basic shape and style of the tank. The paper templates were then transferred in our CAD/CAM program where the actual steel panels were cut. The panels were then carefully shaped and TIG welded together and with a little cutting, pounding and bending, the tank took shape. The students set the tank on the frame numerous times, to be sure it fit, but also to be sure it was going to flow with the bike correctly. Near the end of the tank-fabrication sequence, a pop-up gas cap, donated by Matt Hotch Customs, was installed and welded in.

Once the entire tank was welded and checked for leaks, it was then sent to our painters at Hering Kustoms for a POR 15 seal (thanks to Klock Werks) and the body-filler process began. After a series of sanding/filling sequences, the smooth, satin black paint was applied with some awesome airbrush graphics and old-skool pin striping by Don Hering himself.

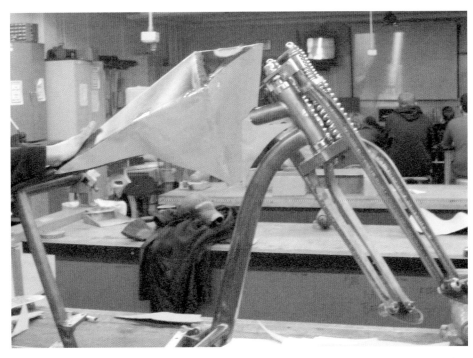

To design the gas tank, the students started by making paper templates of the basic shape.

The templates were then transferred to the CAD system and the pieces were cut out with our CNC plasma cutter.

Clark Davis and Kyle Stelmazek hard at work on the tank. They endured many hours of trial and error getting the tank pieces to fit and weld up just right.

Here's the tank after most of the pieces are finish-welded together. At this point the tunnel still needs to be installed. Good TIG welding skills are very useful in this type of fabrication.

SEAT

The seat was a joint effort of Paul Reagan's aluminum seat pan with a Rock Shox mount, covered with a custom, hand-tooled leather cover by Tim Quick at Outlaw Custom Seats. The seat mounts were lined up and welded on the frame and then ground smooth by the students. This added a unique look that we felt helped give this bike the added wow factor.

FENDER/STRUTS

For the rear fender we decided to use a thirteen dollar trailer fender from Northern Tool. This fender is a very heavy-duty, durable fender that made for a great addition to the bike. After looking at some of the expensive alternatives available, this turned out to be the most affordable solution.

The fender struts were then designed by the students to match the neck gusset and flow with the pointed axle plates. The plan for the struts was to line them up flush with the fender on the bike, and then weld them in place. This would create a clean flow that would make the fender and strut become one. We started by making paper templates of various designs until we came up with one that we really liked. The paper templates were then scanned into the CAD system and after cleaning up the images and getting all dimensions correct, we cut out a set. The struts were cleaned up and then welded to the fender to give it a one-piece look. Be sure to compensate for the chain and any other items that may require the struts to be bent. For the bends we used our hydraulic, 40 ton, iron-worker and were able to easily bend the struts to the needed angles, which gave us the clearance needed.

After finishing the welding of the struts we drilled and threaded the holes in the axle plates where the struts mount. It is recommended to use at least 1/4 - 20, grade 8 bolts oat this point, especially if you plan on having a passenger sitting on the back at any time.

With the tank completed and finally mounted to the frame, the bike started to take shape.

MOTOR/COIL MOUNTS

A matching motor mount and coil bracket, as well as a headlight bracket, were created to match the circles and points seen in the frame. The students began by taking measurements and then making a cardboard template of the basic size and shape they wanted. After the templates were trimmed slightly, the measurements were transferred into our CAD program to be CNC plasma cut from 1/4-inch steel. After all the pieces were cut and checked for proper fit, they could be welded together, and drilled and tapped as needed. Following a little finish work, everything was sent out to Hering Kustoms for a paint job.

This awesome, custom tooled leather work from Tim Quick at Outlaw Custom Seats also incorporated shell casings for a unique look.

A good profile shot of the bike, which shows the smooth lines. The custom made pieces really set the bike apart from the catalog Choppers out on the road.

OIL TANK

A custom Maltese oil tank was donated by Jimmy at Jimmy's Art Shop (Jimmy was killed in a motorcycle accident during the summer of 2005, RIP) and again Hering Kustoms added an old-skool touch with some very nice paint work. The custom oil tank was then mounted to the seat post. This tank does not have a battery box so we had to fabricate one to be mounted behind the transmission. To make this tank fit properly we needed to notch the seat post and mount the tank to the post. Once this was completed, it was rechecked to be sure it was square and in the correct position, and then finally good and tight with Loctite on the bolt threads.

EXHAUST

With the major pieces of the bike assembled and in place the custom pipe fabrication could begin. We had an assortment of old pipes donated from some local bike shops, which would be the foundation for our new custom set. To start the job, the exhaust flanges were cut off and salvaged from an Evo style set of pipes. After the flanges were bolted to the motor securely it was a puzzle to cut, weld, grind and modify to create the style of pipes we wanted. The first attempt at fabricating pipes resulted in a design that just didn't flow real well with the bike's lines. At that point the

The custom rear fender struts, and cut down boat-trailer fender, came together nicely. These are the things that make your bike original and different from the rest.

pipes were cut up and reconfigured to blend better with the overall design. After the pipes were welded and all mounting brackets were attached, they were then taken off to be finished. They were sprayed with a coat of high temperature stove-pipe paint, and then wrapped in some black exhaust wrap. The wrap gives the pipes the old hot rod look while also covering up any imperfections that were left from welding the different pipes together.

CUSTOM FOOT PEGS

We decided to incorporate some of the students' machining skills into the project by having them make a custom set of brass pegs for the forward controls. The students started by taking measurements off a stock set. After the thread size was determined and the proper diameter and length of material was determined, we picked up some brass stock.

The first step was to machine the spiked end onto the peg. After the end was completed the peg was then turned down to the proper outside diameter. Next, the grooves were cut and then we gave the brass a slight polish to clean everything up. The result is a great looking, unique set of pegs. There is a great amount of pride involved in creating your own custom parts, especially when you see the positive reaction you get at shows and events.

We created our own one of a kind motor and coil mount. This design was created to fit with the bikes style and was sure to be something that you couldn't find in any catalog.

A custom-made oil tank from Jimmy was donated to the project. Here it is ready to be installed after Hering Kustoms added some paint and stripes. Due to our tight deadline this tank was painted early in the assembly stage. Because there is no battery box on this tank we needed to figure that out as well.

The custom pipes stated life as set of recycled old drag pipes from a local motorcycle shop. We quickly began chopping them up to create our own design.

REMOTE OIL FILTER

As with all our bikes, we wanted to include a remote oil filter set up. One of the custom Baas Metal Craft, remote oil filter assemblies was welded to the frame, and the big industrial, Fram HP1 filter was added as a tribute to the late Indian Larry. As always these filters add that hard-core race look to any bike, but care should be taken to install the oil lines properly as described in the previous chapter.

TAG MOUNT

The next custom piece was the side-mount license plate/taillight assembly. We wanted, again, to tie the points and circles into this piece and made it fit a donated license plate holder from Eye Candy Customs with the old Cadillac-style taillight. The students created a template of the design they wanted. After creating the piece in the CAD program, it was cut and cleaned up for assembly. We used a mounting system which just slides over the axle and is then bolted tight with the normal outside axle nut. These are available in vertical or horizontal designs. The laws in your state should be checked before you decide which way to run the plate. In certain states it is illegal to run your plate in the vertical position.

The students tried out different designs for the pipes. There are endless ways the exhaust can be run, so be creative and find something that fits the look of the bike.

HEADLIGHT BRACKET

After the mock up was mostly finished, we put the final custom touch on our bike. We wanted the headlight bracket to be something different, but also a part that would flow with the style of the bike. As with the other custom pieces, we started with some sketches and ideas and then created a cardboard template to test the different designs. Once we found the design that best fit the bike it was created in CAD and cut out with our CNC plasma-cutting machine. The final piece was cleaned up and then finally welded on to the front end for a cool custom look.

The final assembly of the finished pipes included welding on the mounting tabs, and wrapping the pipes in black pipe wrap.

FINAL PAINT AND ASSEMBLY

After all the pieces were painted and given the proper curing time, everything was picked up and the final assembly began. All threads were cleaned with the proper taps, the paint was removed from the motor and transmission mounting areas on the frame, and the parts were carefully reinstalled for the last time. Loctite and proper torque specs were used throughout.

WIRING

For the wiring on this bike we used a harness kit from Bitter End, which was donated to our project. All the wires were run inside the frame. What

The custom brass pegs being machined in class by student Clark Davis.

The custom headlight bracket and brass pegs help to give the bike a unique touch. We tried to make as many of the parts for the bike as we could.

The installed remote oil filter assembly. This kit uses a Fram HP1 high flow, low restriction race filter which works nicely with a bike's oil pressure.

follows is a brief description of the wiring work (part of this is taken from the Bitter End installation manual).

When it comes to doing your own wiring, the key word is patience. I started at the starter solenoid. I started here because I find it easy and logical to wire based on the origin of the power - from its source to the subsequent components spread throughout the bike. The large black cable (which may be red – for positive – in other aftermarket cable kits) runs directly from the battery positive to this copper stud on the solenoid. Next, the battery negative, which is wired to the chassis for grounding, is connected. At this point I had a good start on directing power to the rest of the bike. The black wire that runs off in the opposite direction runs up to the copper stud on the 30 amp circuit breaker and is, therefore, the jumping off point for power provided to the rest of the bike (downstream of the starter). The next wire (typically green on stock H-D's and in aftermarket wiring harnesses) runs back to its specific terminal on the starter relay as shown on the diagram.

As mentioned, the cable coming in from the battery negative post runs from the negative battery terminal to a chosen point on the frame. The battery negative can be grounded almost anywhere as long as it is a clean, tight, strong connection to bare steel (or some other conductive metal) that connects to the chassis or frame. A direct connection to the frame is preferable whenever possible.

A clean, secure grounding point is very important to a functional and reliable electrical system. Take your time and do this right the first time. If the battery is not grounded completely, the bike will not be able to take advantage of the full power potential coming from the battery. Given that it may take as little as a one-volt drop to make the starter/solenoid system function erratically – or not at all – this is time well spent.

There are 2 circuit breakers for this wiring system, one is the main 30-amp breaker (look for the actual amperage markings directly on the side of the casing of the breakers). We wire the 30-amp breaker first. Coming in to its copper terminal is the black wire from the copper starter solenoid stud, this is the source of power.

On the silver (outbound) stud of this breaker are three wires. (Note: Service manual schematics will almost always show inbound electrical flow being wired to the copper terminal of a circuit breaker and outbound on the silver stud.) Two of the wires (which will typically be tan in color on stock Harleys and in aftermarket wiring harnesses) provide power to the rest of the bike (one that runs to its specific terminal on the starter relay as shown in the diagram and one that on stock Harley runs to the dash area to feed power to the ignition and light switch.)

The other wire on this terminal is the long (more than three feet in some cases), single black wire that comes from your voltage regulator. The other two wires coming from the regulator plug into

The license plate assembly finished and mounted on the bike. This incorporated an Eye Candy Customs Cadillac style taillight with one of our custom mounting brackets.

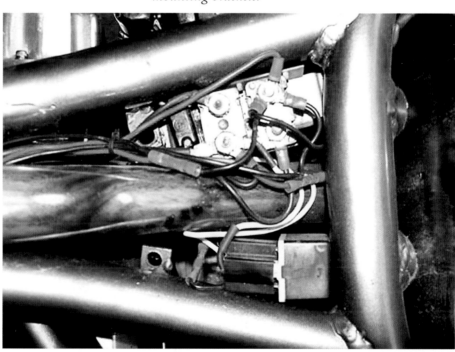

A picture of the Bitter End wiring kit installed on one of their bikes. This is a great way to wire your bike, with easy to follow directions

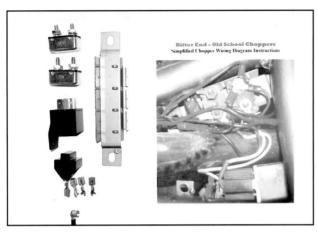

The complete Chopper wiring kit that can be ordered through Bitter End Choppers.

The completed bike after 2 months of hard word and long hours. I couldn't have been more proud of these kids!

The final shot with the core group, Clark Davis, Tyler Thorpe and Kyle Stelmazek.

the stator for the alternator. This stator plug sticks out of the case on the left side.

The power wire coming from the silver terminal (the one not running to the starter relay) runs to the copper stud on the next, 15 amp, circuit breaker. This breaker powers the rest of the accessories on the bike (headlight, taillight, brake lights, and all the rest). Please note: additional circuits and breakers may needed to handle additional accessories (not intended to be covered by the diagram or the kit).

IMPORTANT NOTE ABOUT CIRCUIT BREAKERS

Circuit breakers are extremely important as they protect the electrical system of the motorcycle. Current passes through them as long as they are not "tripped." However, when overloaded, heat causes the circuit breaker to "break" thus preventing a melt down or the harness to catch fire. DO NOT attempt to either bypass or leave the breakers out of the system. Also, take care to make sure that additional breakers are added as necessary so that total circuit amps are less than the rating of the breaker. Conversely, it is important to use a low enough rated breaker that it will trip before damaging levels of heat can build up in the wires.

Next take the little black box, which is the starter relay (included in the kit) and attach it to the relay plug, which merely serves as a gathering and connection point for the various wires that connect to the relay, and a convenient way to plug/unplug all connections at one time.

Also wired to the 30-amp breaker is the black, rectangular backside of a simple toggle switch (easily attainable at almost any local hardware store). These can be wired into any circuit on the bike to turn power on or off to any component (lights, or any other circuit). In our case, it has been wired in series with all the other components so that with the flick of one switch we can control power to the lights, the starter, and the whole bike. Thus, eliminating more wire, and more switches, and more complexity in the system. If hidden cleverly enough, this can also be a theft prevention device since nothing will work if would-be thieves cannot find the hidden switch.

Now, the supply power to the headlight is hooked up and a toggle switch is used to allow for High/Low or off. Keep in mind that some components can be wired to be turned on anytime the ignition is on.

Once a final check of the system was completed and everything on the bike was double-checked, we were ready to fire it up. Before the first start of any bike, be sure every line and hose is routed properly and correctly installed. The fluids should be added following all the manufacturers specifications for type and amounts. Since there are many different types and styles of components, always get the literature for your specific components to be sure you add the correct type and amount of fluid to the engine, transmission and possibly the primary.

THE FINAL SHOW

The class project bike was entered in the Donnie Smith Invitational bike show March 24th and 25th, 2005, in the left-side-drive Evolution motor, rigid frame class. Our bike competed with about 150 other customs and did very well bringing home four awards. The awards included: first place Best Turntable, third place Spectator's Choice, third place Judge's Choice, and third place in our class.

The bike blew away the general public, who had never heard of anything like this being done in a high school. The hand-made pieces and custom fabrication really proved that the kids can put together a true one-of-a-kind custom bike. Many famous faces came by the booth to show their support for what the kids had accomplished. We had the bike lift signed by legends Donnie Smith, Jon Kosmoski, Brian Klock, Dave Perewitz, Kenny Price and Sonny Barger. This was a huge honor for us and it was very exciting for the kids to experience the support and encouragement these and many others gave us. The experience was one to be remembered forever, and has since sparked a new wave of thinking by the educational system with regard to shop classes. Taking this positive experience and using it to help other schools to incorporate the same type of activity into their curriculum will be my top priority in the near future. Support your local high school Chopper class!

THE NEW OWNER

After the show, I displayed the bike at many local Minnesota events as well as bringing it to The Horse, Back Street Choppers Smokey Mountain Smoke Out. The bike fit in well with the garage-built style that Horse followers are into. In the fall, at the start of the 2005/2006 school year, the bike was officially sold to the father of one of the Team Chop project leaders. Clark Davis had been one of the top fabricators and bike builders throughout this project and it's fitting that his father purchased the bike after it was finished.

It was student Clark Davis' father who stepped up and purchased our award winning 2005 school project bike, seen here being loaded up for the trip home.

Chapter Ten

Build Number Three

SPS Kennedy Build

For the 2006 class project we were fortunate to get a large donation from Jeff and Donny at Sucker Punch Sally's. We first heard of these guys a few years ago when the kids were looking for cool ideas for the class builds they were planning. The Sucker Punch web site displayed the exact bike style we wanted, no over stretched bikes, just clean, bare-bones, old-skool rides.

The 2006 Kennedy High School Bobber Build. This bike was built entirely by my Chopper class and was composed of donated parts and hand crafted one-off fabrications.

Right from the start, the folks at SPS supported what we were doing. In fact, they donated a gas tank to last year's build. Later, while at the Smoke Out in 2005, I was able to hang out with them and check out their bikes up close. I was impressed by the quality of the bikes they build and the retro look.

Delivery of the Sucker Punch bike parts was like Christmas for the kids, everything arrived in great shape ready for assembly.

SPS has created the perfect combination of new technology and old skool style. After discussing the new class build at the Smokeout, Jeff and Donny both agreed to help us out again. They agreed to donate one of the SPS no-rake, no-stretch rolling chassis kits. This kit included wheels and tires, all spacers, brakes, oil bag, rear fender, two-under front end, risers, bars, kick stand, sprockets, and tank. Everything was shipped and the build began as the kids opened all the boxes.

This was like a huge party, every box we opened held new, cool parts for the project. This kit has been created to make assembly go quick and error free. All axle spacers are labeled for left and right side and everything bolted together so smoothly that the kids had the entire rolling chassis complete by the next class period!

The students quickly got to work on the frame, pounding in the neck cups.

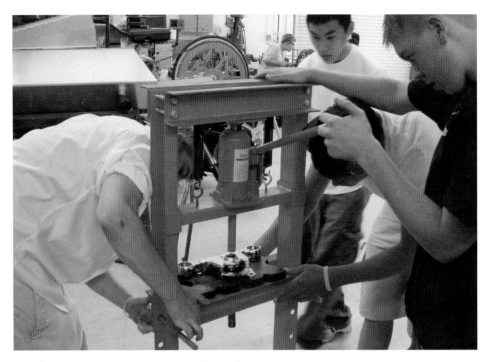

With the help of our shop press the triple trees were fitted with the bearings and dust shield.

After the triple trees were bolted to the frame, the fork legs could be carefully installed. Use caution not to scratch the chrome when you slide them through.

Rolling Chassis

The SPS Deluxe Rolling Chassis kit retails for $3195.00 and includes the following:
- Front and rear wheels & tires
- Fork Assembly with bars and risers
- Headlight and mounting plate
- Gas tank and frame

Options

Options that were added brought the total to $4870.00, and included:
- Side fill oil tank and mounting hardware
- Wernimont rear 8.5 rigid fender
- Forward control
- FXST kick stand
- .500 inch offset 23-tooth sprocket
- Chrome disc sprocket kit
- O-ring chain
- Rear caliper assembly

THE MOCK UP

To assemble this bike you first want to install the neck cups and then set the frame up on a building table, bike lift or where-ever you plan to do the assembly. Make sure it is a solid, safe platform that will allow you to comfortably work on the bike while having it properly secured.

Once we had the rear tire in the frame, the brake caliper could be installed. Because SPS supplied the axle spacers it was easy for the kids to achieve perfect center aliment of the wheel in the frame. This is a huge help for people who do not have access to a lathe (to machine their own custom axle spacers). If you do not have axle spacers, you must take accurate measurements and machine a set to fit, or find someone who will. Many of the parts distributors have axle spacers for sale at almost any size that can be imagined, if you are unable to make them yourself. The supplied two-under, wide-glide front end was then assembled, prior to installation in the frame. The lower dust shield and bearing were pressed on the stem and then the triple trees were installed on the frame. Next, the fork tubes were carefully slipped up into the trees and secured tightly. Now

The frame was made into a roller the same day everything arrived. The SPS working man's special proved to be a great foundation for a trouble free build.

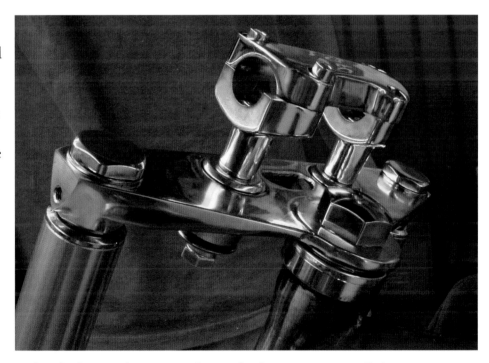

After the front end was secured properly, the risers were installed in preparation for the handlebars.

119

The kit includes all hardware and mounting brackets needed to quickly install almost everything on the bike. Pictured is the complete oil tank kit included in the package deal.

the front wheel can be installed. Again, the supplied wheel spacers made it easy to install the wheel and get it in the dead center of the fork. After the front end is completely installed, we added the proper amount of fork oil to each tube, per manufacturer's recommendation. The risers and bars were installed next.

The bike went from a box of parts to a complete rolling chassis in about an hour. The oil bag supplied with the SPS kit was next on the installation list. This tank comes with all necessary brackets and hardware, no welding or fabrication needed.

The next step on the rolling chassis assembly was to install and mount the rear fender. The fender comes raw, so you can align it, mark it and drill the necessary holes. After drilling the mounting hole in the fender, it was bolted to the frame. With the fender on the bike, it was time to buy or purchase fender struts. For this build we chose to custom create a set of struts that the students designed and cut with our CNC plasma cutting system (more later). This is a great way to add a unique touch to your bike as the number of possible strut designs is endless.

No matter how they look, be sure the struts will clear the chain, and are

With no problems at all the bike was soon on the floor as a rolling chassis. The gas tank, donated by Paul Cox, was then set on and the bike quickly took shape. This bike was built in tribute to Indian Larry. RIP.

120

strong enough that the fender will support a passenger sitting on the back. At a minimum use 1/4-20 bolts for the mounting application. We decided to have our pipes come up behind the oil tank, so the fender was mounted to make room for the tire.

WHEELS AND TIRES

The wheels and tires supplied with our SPS kit included a 21-inch single-flange, 40 spoke front rim matched with a 21 inch Avon Speed Master front tire. The rear is a 16 by 5.5 inch rim with a Dunlop Cruisemax 150/80 B16 white-wall tire. This is a great set up for anyone looking to build an old skool bike with a bit more rear tire width. Anything over 150 is too wide in my opinion. If you want to go totally retro the skinny-tire style bikes can be acquired through Sucker Punch Sally or other good, traditional suppliers.

As this was being built primarily as a display bike we decided to push the hard core, old-style, look. This meant exchanging the single-flange hub and rim for a spool-style hub. The spool hub is a great way to clean up the front end when a front brake is not used.

Note: Eliminating the front brake is not recommended due to safety reasons - the front break supplies well over half of the bike's stopping power.

Here a student installs the brake rotor onto the rear wheel. Use factory torque specs and loc tight on these bolts to ensure a safe bike.

Assembly of the rear wheel with the supplied pre-cut axle spacers made everything go together very easily. Use grease when installing tight fitting components, such as the axles.

Here the controls were laid out before installation. Always inspect and read the manufacturer's directions before installing any component. These were flawless and went on easily.

We also chose not to run a front fender, which is a problem when riding in the rain, but the clean basic bare bones old-skool look we got was worth it. Be aware that running your bike with no front fender creates a lot of spray on wet roads, and that rocks and road debris have a better chance of making their way into your line of sight.

FORWARD CONTROLS

The forward controls supplied with the Sucker Punch roller were a great high quality set that went on very easily. Be aware that when you run such a stock frame setup with the short front end and a jiffy style stand, the bike may sit up too straight and possibly tip over when it's on the kickstand. The SPS team supplied an angled shim designed to sit between the kickstand and frame. The shim changes the angle of the stand and gives the bike more lean so it's much less likely to be knocked over.

Like most of the pieces on this bike, we decided to add our own personal touch to the controls and pegs. Using brass bar stock we created a custom set of pegs, again to showcase the student's fabrication skills. We also decided to run the bike with a suicide jockey shift. This would require us to modify the existing controls (to sup-

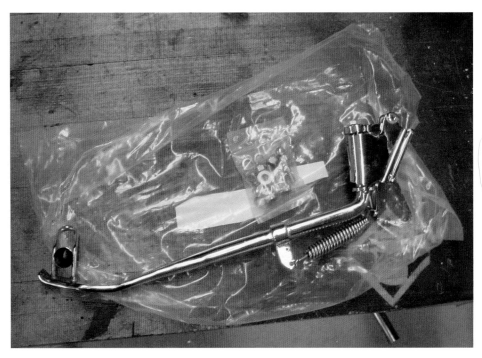

The kick stand with all the needed hardware supplied with the SPS kit.

122

port the clutch cable), build a new set from scratch, or purchase a new set. Fortunately, we were able to get a complete kit from Rick Labroid at Labroid Machine. Rick sold us the complete suicide jockey shift kit that bolted right up to our six-speed transmission, and also had the replacement left forward control with the foot clutch system.

Again a word of caution to any inexperienced rider: It is recommended that you master riding your bike with the traditional hand clutch system before attempting to run a bike with jockey shift.

After looking at the system we decided to fabricate a few pieces so we could retain the SPS forward controls and hook them up to the Labroid foot clutch cable. After a bit of design thought we came up with a system that only required a bolt-on plate and a small, machined, piece that would keep the cable centered. The nearby photo shows how we modified the stock control to accept the suicide clutch cable. After a bit of adjustment and testing the clutch worked very smoothly.

SPARTAN SPRINGER

After the initial mock up of the rolling chassis we were fortunate to get one of Spartan Frameworks cus-

The students used their fabricating skills to machine a set of custom brass pegs for the forward controls. These hand-made pieces really add to a bike.

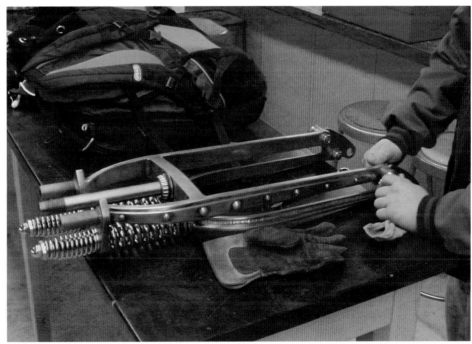

The riveted Spartan Frameworks Springer getting ready to take the place of the wide glide on our project.

tom Springers for the project. This required us to remove the wide glide front fork and install the Springer. The swap was quickly and easily done in less than a half hour. To do this we set the frame up in a way that allowed us to remove the glide front end and install the Springer. The students made sure the frame was blocked up (so the front end can be slipped out from the neck) and secured to the rack or lift. The front end can get

Carefully install the front end, making sure to properly grease, and seat, the bearings and dust shields. Also, use the correct torque recommendations to be sure the front end is installed safely.

a bit squirmy if you do the install by yourself, a helper is definitely a good idea here.

Once the Spartan Springer was installed and tightened to specification, it was time to install the front wheel and tire. One of the problems with spool hubs is the fact that they only come in a 5/8-inch axle. Since we wanted to run a 3/4-inch axle and matching bearings we decided to do a swap to accommodate the bigger axle. To do this we started by removing the old 5/8-inch bearings and inner bearing support sleeve (note the nearby photos). We then took measurements and ordered a new set of 3/4-inch bearings that would fit the hub. The inner support sleeve was then machined and the new sleeve and bearings were installed. Use caution when installing new bearings. If you hit the inner bearing race you can severely damage the bearings. With the new front end and rim set up, we centered the wheel, took measurements, and machined our own custom axle spacers. Next, we created a custom axle on the lathe and

The front end swap was completed quickly and easily, the end result was amazing. This is one of the most unique, high quality, springers I have ever seen.

Old Skool Spool

We start with a spool-hub front wheel with the stock 5/8 inch axle bearings.

Machining the new center spacer to accept the 3/4 inch axle. It's very important to get the size correct.

The bearings are meant for a 5/8 inch axle, the measurement is approximately .609 inches.

Use caution when pounding in new bearings. Do not hit the center race or the bearings will be damaged!

Remove the 5/8 in. axle bearings and center spacer. Use the O.D. dimension from the old bearings to order the new 3/4 in. replacements. Center spacer will also need to be replaced to fit the new axle.

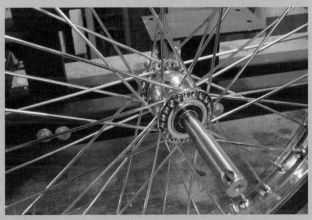

The finished bearing swap with the new axle. Complete kits are available from Baas Metal Craft.

The new Evolution style motor being hand delivered by Elvis, owner of Kokesh Motorcycle. Elvis was kind enough to donate the power plant to the class build. The motor uses H-D internals combined with El Bruto, Mid USA cases.

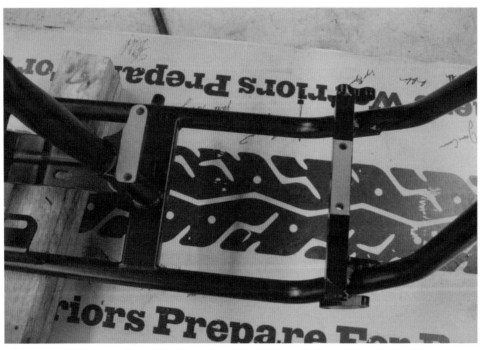

Always remember when installing the motor to carefully remove paint from the surfaces where the motor and transmission will sit. If you do not do this, trouble may be around the corner. As the paint chips away from use you end up with loose bolts and/or worn mounting pads.

used some custom acorn nuts for the ends. The 3/4 inch axle is not necessary but we always like to lean to the safe side, I have seen front axles bent from hitting potholes. The axle spacers were powder coated satin black and the front end was officially complete.

MOTOR AND TRANNY

The motor used on this build was donated by Elvis from Kokesh Motorcycle. This is an El Bruto 80 inch Evolution style motor with all stock Harley-Davidson internal components. After installing the motor in the frame we wanted to give the Evo a bit of an old skool touch. To do this we purchased a used, side mount, Joe hunt magneto (thanks to Fat Boys Grille) and then sent it to Buck at Goblin Millworx for a complete rebuild and some modifications in preparation for installation.

Weyland at Solutions Machining supplied us with the cool machined magneto cover, and with this installed the Evolution motor really picked up an old-skool attitude. To install the motor we carefully placed it in the frame and loosely secured it with the proper mounting bolts. Next, we attached the transmission to the mounting plate on the frame. This SPS frame is great because the six-speed transmission mounted right up to the built-in mounting plate, with no extra transmission plate needed. The inner primary plate can be bolted on next, but there is an alignment sequence to follow.

DRIVELINE ALIGNMENT

Not all frames have perfectly aligned motor and transmission mounts, so you have to be sure the engine, transmission and inner primary are correctly aligned.

First, the motor and transmission must sit square on each mounting point. If the engine sits solid on the mounts, then snug the engine bolts down.

With the engine snug and the tranny loose, the inner primary can be installed and tightened.

Now, look to see if there is space between the transmission and any of the mounting points where the transmission meets the frame. If there is, (you can check the size of the gap with a feeler gauge) the inner primary must be removed so hardened shims can be installed between the tranny case and the mount. The small round shims that come with aftermarket calipers are often useful here. Next, the transmission can be

Aligning the motor and tranny in the frame is very important. If the inner primary doesn't slide off and on easily (after the engine and tranny are tight to the frame), the alignment is not correct and must be corrected.

The motor and tranny properly aligned, and ready for installation of the clutch hub and belt.

Alignment of the rear fender was achieved by laying motorcycle chain along the rear tire for an even spacing and then taping the fender in place to keep it from shifting. Here the bike has a mock-up tank in place as the dished one is already at the painter.

The custom made motor mount with built in key switch housing. The riveted look was incorporated into the students' design to fit the look of the bike.

tightened to the frame and the inner primary re-installed.

Note: if the inner primary won't slide off and on easily with the engine and transmission fully tightened, something isn't aligned correctly and you need to go through the process again.

THE BDL BELT DRIVE

This two-inch belt-drive primary was donated by BDL and came with the custom belt cover. Once the motor and transmission combo were properly aligned and shimmed, we checked all the mounting bolts to be sure everything was tight. The kids installed the pulleys and belt next, and checked for proper tracking. The instructions suggest you use a straight edge across the outside of the pulleys to be sure everything is in proper alignment. If it's not, check your assembly.

We created a custom upper motor mount for our Bobber that would fit with the industrial riveted style used throughout the bike. We made some templates, trying a few different designs, and then came up with the one we thought best fit our theme. We cut the pieces with our CNC system, welded in the rivets, and finished the main piece after test fitting it to the motor. The end slugs were welded on next and the entire piece was TIG welded together, clearcoated and finally installed. The final check of the alignment involves turning over the motor to make sure the belt is tracking correctly. If the belt runs off to one side you will need to check the alignment to find the problem.

FENDER STRUTS

The fender struts we created for this bike were made to match the Springer front end, and work with our riveted industrial design. The struts seemed an ideal place to enhance this look. To position the fender we taped some motorcycle chain over the rear tire, this provided clearance between the finished fender and the tire (the fender can't be too close to the tire because the tire "grows" at speed). We then mounted the fender to the lower transmission mount and secured it with the correct nut and bolt. The fender was then carefully aligned, centered in the frame, and taped down securely so it would not move.

Next, we made sketches of our various strut designs. Once the final design was chosen, cardboard templates we crafted. This would be a double-layered strut, consisting of a 1/2 inch thick piece of steel as the base. On top

Here the students use the mill to drill the bottom of the fender struts in preparation for the tapping process.

After the holes were machined, we tapped the holes to accept 1/4 - 20 bolts which would mount the fender strut to the frame. Always be patient when using a tap, you don't want to break one off in the hole.

After the struts were completed, the fender was attached and mounted on the bike. The hidden mounting points really cleaned up the look of the rear fender, with all bolts hidden behind and underneath the fender.

of that we would add a 1/4 inch riveted piece so the strut would match the look of the front fork. Once we had a template we liked, the dimensions were transferred into the CAD program. The steel pieces were cut out with the CNC mill, using a thinner 12-gauge steel just to test the design. Once we knew the shape was exactly what we wanted, the final struts were cut out from 1/2 inch and 1/4 inch material. Next, we determined the rivet spacing, and the holes were marked and drilled to accept the rivets. We drilled straight through both pieces of the strut material, and welded the rivets in from the backside, which secured the two pieces together securely.

The struts were then attached to the frame and holes were drilled from the inside of the fender into the struts. We tapped these holes to allow for a clean hidden fender mount. We wanted to keep the bare steel look on the struts so we made them detachable from the frame. This way when the frame went out to paint, the struts could be clear powder coated (by SE Custom Powder Coating).

In order to make the struts detachable, we welded some steel mounting pieces to the frame and then drilled up through

The custom remote oil filter bracket, with more rivets incorporated into the design. After the bracket was welded to the frame the filter assembly could be installed. This oil filter system adds a hard-core look to any bike.

those pieces into the strut. After running a tap into the holes in the strut, we were able to cleanly bolt the struts to the frame and then to the fender, with no visible mounting points. After some minor clean up with a belt sander the struts were complete, and really added a cool custom touch to the look of the bike.

GAS TANK

For the gas tank we received one of the cool, dished Mustang tanks from Paul Cox and Indian Larry Legacy. This tank has the ultimate old skool look, and we were honored to receive the tank. Indian Larry and Paul used this style tank on many of their old skool bike builds, and for good reason - it is just a very cool piece. The tank was modified in a few ways to allow the student's to exercise their fabrication and design skills. First, one of Joe McGlynn's Speedster gas caps from Crime Scene Choppers was installed.

To do this we first had to cut out the old gas cap mount. We did this by creating a plug from wood, which was inserted into the gas opening (note the nearby pictures) and then cutting the old cap out using a metal hole saw (we borrowed the technique from Bandit on bikernet.com). The new speedster cap was

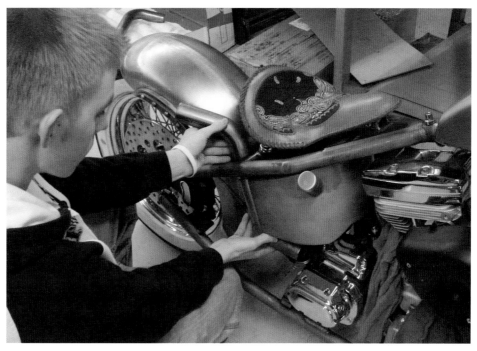

Students used a little trial and error as they looked at different ways to create a custom exhaust. This style, coming up and out behind the seat, was inspired by Billy Lane. The seat shown was donated by Outlaw Custom Seats.

Thanks to Basani Exhaust and Sampson Exhaust, we had plenty of raw pipe to work with when the exhaust fabrication began.

To start the process we used some old scrap head pipes attached to the motor. This began the puzzling process of matching pieces to get the desired design.

Here you can see the evolution of our exhaust system.

then TIG welded into place. This cap is a unique sand-cast piece that has the antique look of an old vintage artifact, with high quality brass screws and stainless hinges.

The riveted industrial look was used as we created a set of standoff steel rings with rivets for the dished sides of the tank. To do this we again created a cardboard template and then transferred the dimensions into our CAD/CAM program. After cutting out the 12 gauge samples, and making modifications, we were then ready to make the rings from the final 1/4-inch steel material. The holes for the rivets were laid out with the CAD program and cut out at the same time as the rings. After the two pieces were cut they were cleaned up, ready for installation of the rivets.

We decided to use our TIG welder and weld the rivets from the backside. After all the rivets were welded in, the excess material was cut off and the backside was ground smooth. We then drilled the holes for the stand off mounting points and created four standoff slugs for each plate that would be welded to the tank. After the holes were drilled in the rings, and the stand

The new oil tank assembly, with the stainless steel battery box TIG welded up along with one of the end caps.

A finished end cap tack-welded in place on the oil tank.

The finished oil tank installed on the bike, again the riveted look really tied in well with the industrial look of the bike.

The gas tank was going to get one of the retro styled, speedster gas caps from Crime Scene Choppers. To begin the tank's transformation, we first made a plug from wood to help keep the hole saw straight as we cut out the old cap mount.

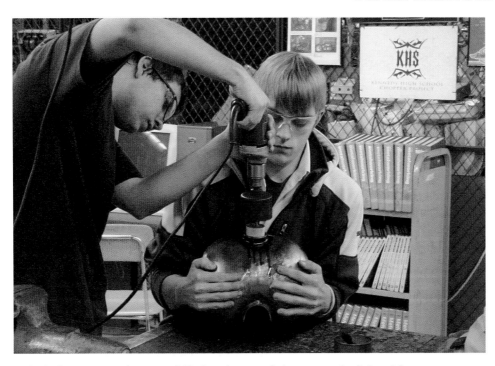

The hole saw was then carefully lined up and the removal of the old cap mount was completed. Use plenty of cutting oil and take your time while drilling.

offsets were machined, the pieces were screwed together, and then set on the tank to be TIG welded on. A few minor grinding modifications were needed to get the stand off to sit level, and at the right height. Once the correct spacing was achieved, the stand offs were tack welded on to the tank. Be careful not to burn through the gas tank wall when welding, you don't want to create any possible leak areas on the tank. The rings were then unbolted from the stand off and finish-welded to the tank. After the stand offs were secured the tank was cooled and the riveted rings were reattached and checked for proper fit. One side became a bit distorted from the welding so the screws had a hard time going in. Rather than risk breaking one off or stripping the threads, we drilled out the holes a little and then the spacer mounted smoothly.

HANDLEBARS

For the handlebars we had three options for this build. The first set came from Colin at Cooper Customs. These are a set of his custom Drunk n Monkey bars which will definitely make your old-skool ride stand out. The bars are fabricated by Colin from high quality material and have a unique style that is sure to get the attention of spectators. These bars have a unique look to them and are rather deceiving. They seem to be extremely tall and possibly hard to reach because of the design and the large diameter tubing. In reality they fit me perfectly, and I am not a tall person at all, being five-foot eight. The second set of bars were the straight broomstick style. This simple bar is said to be tough on the wrists, but they definitely have a unique, clean, cool look to them. These consisted of just a piece of 1-inch stock, cut down to the desired length, clamped into the dog-bone risers.

Finally, the third set is a traditional mid-ape handle bar mounted with the dog bone risers. These are the clean classics you see on many of the old style bikes of yesterday and today. Their timeless style has been around for a long, long time and will surely be with us for years to come.

OIL TANK

Once the riveted look of the bike started to take over, we decided to carry the theme into the oil tank. For this we contacted Dustin at Lucky Charm Choppers. He supplied us with an awesome build-your-own kit for a stainless steel dished riveted tank. This kit supplied us with everything we needed to assemble the unique dished, riveted oil tank shown. The parts in this kit all came clearly marked and the assembly was very easy to do. A TIG welder is needed to weld the stainless. If this is not an option, Dustin can also supply you with a fully built one.

After removing the old oil tank, we placed the new one in place to check the mounting. There were a few minor adjustments needed after we welded on the mounting tabs, but overall the tank swap was very easy. The existing oil tank mounts needed to be cut off and the rear bracket was relocated and re-used. The front bracket was cut off for good and two new tabs were created to secure the tank from the top. After the mounting was completed, we were very happy with the overall appearance of the oil

The new cap-mount tack-welded in place with the TIG welder. Check the cap for proper alignment before you finish the welding.

The finished product. A wicked-cool, dished Mustang tank from Indian Larry Legacy, and the cool speedster gas cap, make for a tank like no other.

We chose the brass mounting hardware on this cap to match the brass pegs the students created. There is also a stainless steel version of this cap.

After the tank was mounted we decided to add one more custom touch. Riveted rings were designed and created with our CNC plasma cutting system. The rings were cut and then the rivets were welded on from the back side of the ring.

The finished ring with mounting holes drilled, and counter sunk, in preparation for mounting on the tank. The rivets and panel are carbon steel. The rings were then clear powder coated by SE Customs.

tank. It is something that fit the bike perfectly and will be used on many of our future bikes.

We also wanted to modify the oil system to incorporate the big HP1 remote oil filter kit. This kit is available through BAAS Metal Craft and each mounting bracket can be custom made to fit the bike. I designed this bracket to incorporate the riveted look but yet be a clean, low-key piece. The final product gives the bike an industrial, Indian-Larry inspired look. To add another unique touch we decided to run copper oil lines. These lines really dress up the look of the bike, and give it one of those custom details that everyone notices right away.

SEAT

We had two choices for this bike. Paughco and Tim Quick teamed up again to create the cool bandana seat, which they donated right from the start of the project. This seat is a great piece, but after the riveted style stared taking over the kids wanted to try something different. The second seat is one I created with the leather work of Duane Ballard Leather. I started with one of my old-skool style, stainless steel seat pans. I then added the copper rivets along the edges of the seat pan. After my pan was completed, and the mounting hardware was installed, I sent the seat to Duane who had full control over the design of the leather work. He knew the basic color, and the style of the bike, which guided him to create this leather work of art. The color of the leather really went well with the paint scheme, and the rivets really worked well with the rest of the bike. After putting both seats on the finished bike, the kids voted that the riveted one was a must.

EXHAUST PIPES

For the exhaust we decided to make a custom set of our own design. After brainstorming a few ideas we decided to go with a unique set of pipes that would come up behind the starter and oil tank, and through the frame behind the seat and fender. To start, we took an old set of used Evolution style pipes and cut them off. After bolting the pipe-ends to the motor, the task of creating pieces to finish the exhaust began. For this we used a combination of old pipe pieces and some new sections donated by Kenny Price

Near the end of the mock-up process with the old tank still on the bike. A thorough mock up paves the way for a trouble free final assembly.

While we were in the design stages a few bar styles were tested. The students picked these crazy Drunk'n Monkey bars from Cooper Customs. At this point we were waiting for the sheet metal to come back from the painter.

137

We painted the one-off pipes, and then wrapped them in thermal tape.

at Samson exhaust. Different pieces were gathered, to create the needed bends, and shaped to work the exhaust around the transmission and up behind the fender. The finished exhaust would turn out right behind the seat. We had room for the pipes between the fender and the seat cross post, due to the way we mounted the fender. In fact, this turned out to be a great way to fill the void there. After a few tries we finally got the pipes to run exactly the way we wanted. This meant we could fabricate the mounting tabs that would mount the pipes and hold them securely. The welds were then ground down in preparation for some black stove pipe paint, and finally the heat wrap.

FINAL TOUCHES

After the mock up was completed we double-checked the entire bike for any details that might have been missed. A Fab Kevin side mount taillight was added, and then the entire bike was torn apart for paint. Hering Kustoms of Northfield, Minnesota again took care of the paint on this build. Don Hering is one of the best painters in the world and always amazes us with his top quality work. The paint for this bike is a deep gold with a heavy

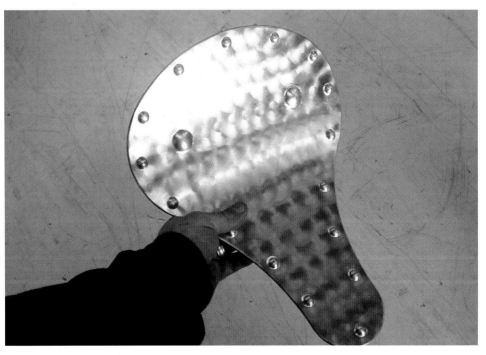

We decided to use one of the Baas Metal Craft, stainless steel, riveted seat pans, as it fit the style of the bike. The seat pan was then sent to Duane Ballard Leather for a custom cover.

metalflake. The flake mixed with the traditional hot rod old-skool pin striping really sets this bike off as a vintage-style ride. The paint, mixed with the raw steel accents created a look for this bike that I have never seen on any other motorcycle. After completion of the build we again were invited to the Donnie Smith Invitational bike show.

Our bike received great reviews and was voted by the professional judges as the winner of the technical merit award for the kid's creativity and fabrication skills. To see the amazement in the spectator's eyes as they realized that this bike was created by a group of high skool kids was awesome. This bike will be on display again at various events and then sold in fall. Don't forget to Support your local high school Chopper class!

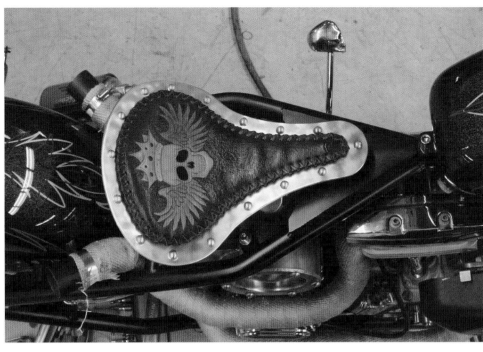

The finished seat after Duane Ballard tooled the leather and attached the pad. This made for a very unique seat.

Nearly finished. The final assembly is exciting, but also a lot of work.

Copper oil lines were used on the bike. These require a great deal of patience and skill to get them to fit and function properly.

After most of the final assembly was completed, the bike really took on a look unmatched by any other. This head turner would definitely not get lost in the crowd at the various biker events.

Here is the finished gas tank after Hering Kustoms applied the wicked old-skool striped and flaked paint job. This paint job looks incredible in the sun and really catches the eye of spectators.

With the bulk of the final assembly finished, including the plumbing and cables, our creation is ready for the Donnie Smith Bike Show.

Wolfgang Books On The Web
www.wolfpub.com

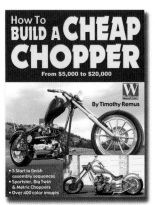

HOW TO BUILD A CHEAP CHOPPER

Choppers don't have to cost $30,000. In fact, a chopper built from the right parts can be assembled for as little as $5,000. *How to Build a Cheap Chopper* documents the construction of 4 inexpensive choppers with complete start-to-finish sequences photographed in the shops of Donnie Smith, Brian Klock and Dave Perewitz.

Least expensive is the metric chopper, based on a Japanese 4-cylinder engine and transmission installed in an hardtail frame. Next up, price wise, are 2 bikes built using Buell/Sportster drivetrains. The recipe here is simple, combine one used Buell, or Sportster, with a hardtail frame for an almost instant chopper. The big twin chopper is the least cheap of the 4, yet it's still far less expensive than most bikes built today.

Twelve Chapters   144 Pages $24.95   Over 400 photos-100% color

---

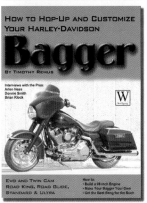

HOW TO HOP-UP AND CUSTOMIZE YOUR HARLEY-DAVIDSON BAGGER

Baggers don't have to be slow, and they don't have to look like every other Dresser in the parking lot. Take your Bagger from slow to show with a few more cubic inches, a little paint and some well placed accessories.

Written by well-known author Tim Remus, How to Hop Up & Customize your Bagger shows you how to upgrade the engine, lower the bike, and personalize the paint and sheet metal. Over 400 color images help explain exactly what it takes to install a set of springs in the front forks, or re-program the fuel injection map.

Follow along as the project bike, a 2004 Standard, makes the transition from stock to custom: including an upgrade to 95 cubic inches, and the addition of a flamed paint job laid out over the standard black urethane.

Eight Chapters   144 Pages $24.95   Over 400 photos - 100% color

---

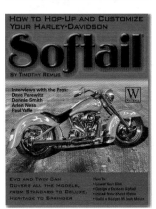

HOW TO HOP-UP AND CUSTOMIZE YOUR HARLEY-DAVIDSON SOFTAIL

Got a Softail? Got a hankering to separate yours from all the other Softails parked outside the bar? Search no farther than this new book, How To Hop-Up and Customize Your Harley-Davidson Softail, from well-known author Timothy Remus. Whether your goal is to personalize that two-wheeled ride or give it more than 60 horsepower, the ideas and answers you need are right here.

Learn how to install a 95 inch kit with over 100 horsepower, add a 250 rear tire, lower the bike, and add extended fuel tanks. Included are customizing ideas, start to finish photo sequences of engine, chassis and paint work, and a list of suppliers for lights, engine hop-up parts, paint and chrome accessories.

The various Softail models are among the most popular bikes ever built in Milwaukee. Make yours faster, sexier and more personal with this all-color book from Tim Remus and Wolfgang Publications.

Nine Chapters   144 Pages $24.95   500 color images - 100% color

---

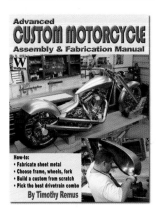

ADVANCED CUSTOM MOTOCYCLE ASSEMBLY AND FABRICATION

It all started in the mid-90s when a few people decided to build their own bike from aftermarket parts. Today, every small town has a Custom bike shop, and every motorhead wants to build a sexy softail like the ones they see on TV.

Wolfgang Publications and Tim Remus were there at the very beginning, and they're back with Advanced Custom Motorcycle Assembly & Fabrication. Part catalog, part service manual, and part inspiration, this new book offers help with planning the project, getting the right look, fabricating parts and assembling that custom bike you've been dreaming about.

Three start-to-finish sequences, with builders like Donnie Smith and Dave Perewitz, show not just how the best bikes are bolted together, but how the unique one-off gas tanks are shaped and then fitted to the stretched soft-tail frames.

Nine Chapters   144 Pages $24.95   Over 400 color images - 100% color

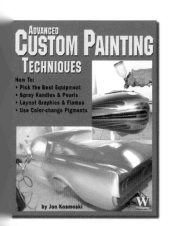

Sources

250 Engineering
937-492-1900

Accurate Engineering
128 Southgate Road
Dolhan, AL 36301
334-702-1993

American Thunder
Custom Motorcycles
1244 Hwy 13 South
Savage, MN 55378
877-389-0138 - 952-746-7786
www.americanthunder.us

Baas Metal Craft
www.baasmetalcraft.com

Bassani Exhaust
www.bassani.com

Belt Drives Ltd.
1959 North Main St.
Orange, CA 92865
www.beltdrives.com

Bikers Choice
www.bikerschoice.com
812-752-5182

Bitter End - Old School Choppers
3004 S Lake Rd S
Scottsburg IN 47170
812-752-5182
www.bitterendchoppers.com

Black Label Frame Works
260-747-8336

Broadway Choppers
1518 Bradley St.
Schenectady, NY 12305
518-374-0008
www.broadwaychoppers.com

Choppers Inc.
www.choppersinc.com

Chrome Hardware Supply
www.chromehardwaresupply.com

Cooper Customs
563-382-0206
www.coopercustoms.com

County Line Choppers
315-593-2992
www.countylinechoppers.com

Crime Scene Choppers
831-406-0126
www.crimescenechoppers.com

Dirty South Choppers
www.dirtysouthchoppers.com

Donnie Smith Custom Cycles Inc.
10594 Radisson Rd. NE
Blaine, MN 55449
763-786-6002
Fax: 763-786-0660
www.donniesmith.com

Duane Ballard Custom Leather
36 Goen Rd.
New Ipswich, NH 03071
603-781-7505
www.dbcustomleather.com/

Dumbassbiker.com
1598 E. Shore Drive
St. Paul, MN 55106
612-296-7771
www.dumbassbiker.com

Exile Cycles
www.exilecycles.com

Fab Kevin
www.fabkevin.com

Fat Boys Bar & Grille
www.fatboysmn.com

Flathead Power -U.S.
8412 Hwy. 182, Suite 100
Morgan City, Louisiana 70380
985-385-2244
www.flatheadpower.com

Flyrite Choppers
13200Pond Springs RD #B-12
Austin TX, 78729
512-918-chop
www.flyritechoppers.com

Ghostriders
www.ghostridersinc.com

GMA Engineering
www.gmabrakes.com

Goblin Millworx
843-200-1563
www.goblinmillworx.com

Hering Kustoms
2822 100th St E.
Northfield, MN 55057
507-645-7065
www.heringkustoms.com

Hot Match Custom Cycles
www.hotmatchcustomcycles.com

Indian Larry Legacy
151 N 14th Street
Brooklyn, NY 11211
718-609-9184
www.indianlarry.com
www.paulcoxleather.com

Jammer Cycle products
1-800-597-6467
www.jammerclub.com

Kendall Johnson Customs
4629 South Main Street
Winston Salem NC 27127
www.kendalljohnsoncustoms.com

Klock Werks
915 S. Kimball
Mitchell, SD 57301
605-996-3700
www.kustomcycles.com

Kokesh Motorcycle
8302 Hwy 65
Spring Lake Park, MN 55432
763-786-9050
www.kokeshmotorcycle.com

Kustomwerks
1200 South Park Dr.
Kernersville, NC 27284
Inquiries: 336-996-8690
www.kustomwerks.com

La Briola Machine
303-433-8785
www.lajockeyshifter.com

Lee's Speed Shop
12450 Highway 13 So.
Savage, MN 55378
952-233-2782
www. Leesspeedshop.com

Lucky Charm Choppers
618 Markley Street
Norristown, PA 19401
610-275-9200

Lucky's Garage
www.luckys-garage.com

Maverick Customs
www.maverickcustoms.com

Northern Tool & Equipment
www.northerntool.com

Outlaw Custom Seats
1410 Hidden Circle Drive
Sugar Hill, GA 3051
770-271-1745
www.outlawcustomseats.com

POR 15
www.por15.com

Pruno MFG
www.prunomfg.com

Renegades Bar & Grille
www.renegadesbarandgrill.com

Samson Exhaust
www.samsonusa.com

SE Custom Powdercoating
www.secustompowdercoating.com
952-890-7373

S&S Cycle, Inc.
14025 County Hwy. G
Viola, Wisconsin 54664
608-627-2080
www.sscycle.com

Solutions Machining & Welding
2844 Stirling Road, Suite L
Hollywood, Florida 33020
954-816-6646
www.solutionsmachining.com

Spartan Frameworks
829 E. 17th. St.
Tucson, Arizona 85719
Toll Free: 877-877-5499
www.spartanframeworks.com

Sucker Punch Sally
Miamitown, Ohio 45041
513-353-2803
www.suckerpunchsallys.com

Spyke
www.spyke1.com

TBear Wear
Attire with Attitude
www.tbearwear.com

Ted Tine Motorsports
244 Middlesex Turnpike
Chester, CT 16412
860-526-2060
www.tedtine.com

Terry's Custom
241 E. 4th street
Latham, IL 62543
217-674-3469
www.terry-zone.com

The Horse Backstreet Choppers
www.ironcross.net

Toxic Cycle, Inc.
5385 W. Hwy 13
Savage, MN 55378
952-895-8883

Two-Bit Choppers
Milliken, CO 80543
970.587.5867
www.twobitchoppers.com

Wimmer Custom Cycle
www.wimmermachine.com

Young Choppers & Hot Rods
www.youngchoppers.com